Rochelle Melander and Harold Eppley

The Spiritual Leader's Guide to Self-Care

FOREWORD BY ROY W. OSWALD

An Alban Institute Publication

Library of Congress Catalog Number 2002104638
ISBN 1-56699-262-1

For our dear daughter Eliana,
whose arrival in the midst of writing this book
reminded us that taking care of ourselves
is more important than ever.

Contents

Foreword

What do you look for in a spiritual leader, one you would want to serve as your spiritual guide? Certainly you would want such a guide to have some knowledge and insight into the life of the spirit. I suspect you would want this person to manifest a life of peace and joy and to be a genuinely caring person. You would also want this person to be authentic and to have personal insight into his or her own behavior, thoughts, and feelings. And you would want to see evidence that this spiritual guide practices good self-care.

It is not often that I see the words "spiritual" and "self-care" in the same sentence. For various reasons, we find it hard to put those two concepts together. We often think of the spiritual journey in terms of worship and service. For the most part, however, we confuse self-care with self-indulgence. Rare is the spiritual leader who sees self-care as a matter of worship and service as well as a central ingredient for being an effective pastor.

Rochelle Melander and Harold Eppley offer us a real gift in this book, a tool for thinking about what is required of a spiritual guide. In a practical way, they invite us to examine this "being" side of our life and role and invite us into a more holistic way of being a spiritual leader. Rather than talking about the trappings of ministry, they focus on the essence of being a true spiritual guide.

For the past 26 years, as a senior consultant with the Alban Institute, I have tried to invite clergy into greater self-care. I consider my book *Clergy Self Care: Finding a Balance* to be one of the more important books I have written. Yet, as I deal with hundreds of clergy each year in workshops and seminars around the country, I continue to observe that at least 20 percent of them are severely burned out. Another 50 percent are clearly bordering on burnout and are already manifesting some of the ill effects of this malaise. My assessment is that the core of this debilitating disease among ordained people is our tendency to focus on *doing* rather than on *being*.

Polarity management, a concept developed by organizational development consultant Barry Johnson, is one useful tool for helping us understand this doing-being tension. A polarity is an unsolvable problem that can only be managed. There is both an upside and a down side to each pole of the problem, and the two poles are inseparable in that the down side of one pole is answered by the upside of the opposite pole. On a polarity map, the doing-being polarity would look something like this:

+	+
Exploring ministry opportunities	Rest, revitalization, and spiritual renewal
Visiting the sick	Gaining perspective
Offering pastoral care and counseling	Acknowledging one's limitations
Leading the board and congregation	Enjoying God's acceptance and grace
Being strong for others	Accepting oneself
Being an advocate for the Holy	Being grounded in one's authentic self
Witnessing to one's faith	Remembering who we are
DOING	**BEING**
-	-
Burnout	Spiritual narcissism
Overextending oneself	Becoming over-focused on one's self
Neglecting one's own needs	Isolation
Neglecting friends and family	Navel gazing
Becoming cynical	Loss of concern for others
Being overwhelmed by problems	Loss of sense of mission
Becoming exhausted and humorless	Hypochondria
Physical/emotional illness	Becoming part of the "me" generation
Being at one's worst	Excessive self-absorption

As is obvious in this polarity, the down side of *doing* leads to burnout, exhaustion, cynicism, and disillusionment. This is only answered by the upside of *being*. We can, of course, overemphasize *being*, which is a kind of narcissism and self-absorption. The only way out of this hole is to go do something for someone else. Yet, before we go back to the *doing* pole, can we see how necessary it is for spiritual leaders to spend time on the *being* side of this polarity?

Those seeking to be healthy spiritual leaders and to draw the best practices from this "doing-being" polarity will find a real gift in this book. What is unique about it is that the authors rarely talk about spirituality and self-care in the abstract. Every chapter offers the reader practical activities that will lead us to balance and wholeness. There is no way anyone will be able to take these assignments seriously without experiencing a transformed way of living and doing ministry.

Readers will also love Melander's and Eppley's holistic approach to the balanced life. Up for examination are one's life vision, faith journey, authentic self, and daily practices and priorities; one's care of the body, soul, spirit, relationships, finances, and living space; and leaving a legacy. We know, too, they have strayed from the mainstream of the religious world when they advocate "cultivating delight."

The book is also a treasure trove of designs that church professionals can use to encourage congregants to move their lives towards greater wholeness through self-examination and self-affirmation. The price of the book is worth the 25 pages of annotated bibliography, which includes numerous Web sites to explore for everything from information on spiritual direction, meditation, and visualization, to exercise and fitness. One cannot help but be impressed with the breadth of material these two have explored and digested. I am grateful these two have made the sacrifices they have to put this book in print. I am confident you will be too.

ROY M. OSWALD
Senior Consultant
The Alban Institute

Preface

Just What Is Self-Care?

In the oft-quoted rabbinic story, Rabbi Zusya says to his students, "In the next life, I shall not be asked: 'Why were you not Moses or Isaac or Jacob?' I shall be asked: 'Why were you not Zusya?'"* Self-care involves more than eating a balanced diet and regularly visiting the doctor. Self-care means living the life God has intended for you. You are God's own creation. Your task is to be yourself, the person God has called you to be. This includes creating a vision for your life and then crafting a life that honors that vision. It includes caring for your body, mind, spirit, and the resources God has given to you. Caring for yourself means that in the next life, you will be able to say to God, "I was very much myself, your own creation."

Why We Wrote This Book

We are not paragons of self-care—just the opposite. As a clergy couple, we have spent many years struggling to care for ourselves and our family while faithfully attending to our duties as parish pastors. It is an ongoing struggle. Some weeks we fail to keep our priorities straight, we don't pray as often as we need to, and we both have a weakness for potato chips.

Our primary challenge has been learning that caring for ourselves is part of how we minister to others. As spiritual leaders, we know that others are watching our actions closely. Imagine a pastor who speaks of family values, but attends church functions five nights a week instead of spending time with his family. Imagine a parish educator who teaches "love your neighbor as yourself," but doesn't take time to properly eat or sleep. Imagine a church musician who encourages her choir members to follow God's call and yet has never pursued her own life's vision—to publish her music. What you do reveals much more about what you believe than what you say.

We have also discovered that taking care of ourselves enables us to minister better with others. If you have ever traveled on an airplane, you have probably heard a flight attendant's reminder that in case of a loss of air pressure you should attach your own oxygen mask before attempting to assist others. Caring for yourself is like attaching an oxygen mask. You are able to minister to others because your own needs are being met.

Finally, we have learned that self-care is not a solitary endeavor. Left to our own devices, most of us fall victim to inertia. We need God's grace and the ongoing encouragement of others to prod us toward health. We hope that this book will serve as an instrument of God's grace for you, a source of inspiration as you seek to care for yourself.

This book addresses issues that are common to all humans, as well as many that are specific to the unique lifestyle of spiritual leaders. We understand the term "spiritual leader" to include clergy of all faiths as well as parish administrators, educators, counselors, music directors, and others who hold leadership roles in congregations or faith-based organizations.

A Coaching Perspective

The exercises in The Spiritual Leader's Guide to Self-Care encourage and prod you to improve your life and ministry, sometimes by asking you to gain knowledge about yourself and your situation and sometimes by challenging you to take action.

This book approaches self-care from a coaching perspective. It is about making and embracing changes, maintaining well-being, and fixing problems in the present and the future. Once information is gleaned, the question is always, "Now what?" In this way, coaching is quite different from therapy, which often delves into one's past and one's emotional history. Although we do occasionally ask that you look at your past, this book is not meant to replace therapy. If at any time during the course of using this book you feel anxious, depressed, or suicidal, contact a therapist or local help line immediately.

Staying Connected

Working through the exercises in this book will involve making a number of life changes. You will work to redefine yourself and how you function in your world. As a result, you may meet with resistance from some of your family, friends, colleagues, and the people you serve. As you remain focused on these important life changes, work at staying connected to the people you care about.

- Identify key people in your life and in the community you serve who you know will support you in making life changes. Share with them your intent to work through the exercises in this book and ask them to commit to support you through prayer in the next year. You might want to ask if they will meet with you regularly to celebrate your successes and encourage you when you meet with resistance.
- Encourage those you love in their own journeys of growth.
- Invite family, friends, and colleagues to work through appropriate exercises with you.
- You may need to limit contact with those persons who are openly hostile or critical of the changes you are making to care for yourself.

Staff Support Committees

Since many of the changes you will be making will affect the environment in which you work, you will want to seek the support of the community you serve. A staff support committee can be a helpful link between you and your congregation. This committee can serve as advocates for you as you seek to take better care of yourself. Talk to them about your intentions. Ask them for their ongoing support and prayers. If possible, involve them in the process by sharing some of the book's exercises with them. There are helpful resources in the appendix under both "committees" and "staff support committees" to help you work with this group.

How to Use This Book

Weekly Format

The Spiritual Leader's Guide to Self-Care is organized into 52 weeks of exercises, including six retreat weeks. You can work through the weeks in order over the course of the year or you can vary the pattern according to your needs. You may want to work only with the chapters that suit you, or you may prefer to spend two or three weeks on chapters that you find especially helpful or that need more of your attention.

Each regular week contains these sections:

- *A Brief Introduction*
- *Connecting with Yourself*
  This section includes journaling exercises and personal activities designed to help you reflect on the weekly theme. At the beginning of each week, take time to read through this section and plan to set aside enough time during the week to work through it. Use your journal in a way that works for you. You might choose to include prose, poetry, or song verses. You might also use visuals such as coloring, painting, drawing, or sculpting.
- *Connecting with a Partner*
  This section provides questions and exercises to be done with a colleague and serves as reinforcement to the self-reflection and activities you do on your own. As we mentioned earlier, self-care is not a solitary endeavor. Seek out a colleague who is committed to self-care and with whom you will be able to meet over the course of a year. It is best if you can meet with someone face to face. If this is not possible, adapt the exercises to meet your needs. You might meet over the phone and supplement your conversations with e-mail correspondence.

When you meet with a group of colleagues. We recommend keeping the size of the group to four participants or less so that everyone will have an adequate amount of time for reflection.

When you meet, set up the ground rules for your sessions. Here are some that we have found helpful:

— Agree to meet at a regular time.
— Agree to keep your conversations confidential.

— Agree to take turns listening and speaking, perhaps using a time limit of 10 minutes each.

— Agree to listen to your partner without trying to solve his or her problems.

- *Connecting with God*
  The popular adage "work like it all depends on you, pray like it all depends on God" applies to self-care as well. We encourage you to connect with God in a way that relates to the weekly theme. Adapt these exercises to your own faith tradition or comfort level.

- *Challenge*
  This section wraps up the theme of the week's activities with a concrete action that you can take to care for yourself or improve your life.

Retreat Weeks

Retreat weeks occur at the end of every section. They are designed to allow you a further opportunity to reflect upon the material within the previous section by creating your own retreat structure. They provide some guidance regarding resources and activities, but the content of retreats is up to you.

We encourage scheduling your retreat for two nights, allowing one full day. If this is not possible, schedule whatever time you can—anything from two hours to an entire day. Getting away from your daily life and ministry settings is the key to a successful retreat. Make sure you disconnect yourself from the conveniences that make you accessible to the outside world—your cell phone, pager, computer, and handheld.

Retreats give you the opportunity to reflect on your life from a new vantage point and without the usual daily distractions. You do not need to travel far. If you choose an overnight retreat, you might stay at a hotel, bed and breakfast, retreat center, monastic community, convent, a friend's home, or a campground. If you take time during a day, try visiting a local library, a bookstore, a park, a beach, a coffee shop, a neighboring church, a museum, or any other place that offers a retreat-like setting for you. The resource list at the end of the book offers suggestions for retreat materials and places.

A Final Word of Encouragement

We applaud you for taking the time and energy to make changes in your life. Caring for yourself—God's own creation—is holy work. It is never selfish. Caring for yourself ensures that the people you serve will be blessed with a healthier, more whole spiritual leader. As you work through the exercises in this book, you will sometimes stumble or even fail. But don't give up! Give yourself the permission to start again. Keep moving forward— at any pace that works for you. Remember that the journey of a thousand miles begins with a single step.

---

*   Rabbi Zusya, quoted in *The Cloister Walk* by Kathleen Norris (New York: Riverhead, 1996), 63.

Acknowledgments

This book exists because the staff at the Alban Institute understands that spiritual leaders need to care for themselves in order to be effective caregivers for others. We thank our editor, Beth Ann Gaede, for her enthusiastic support of our proposal and for her wise guidance throughout the process of creating this book.

Many people provided assistance in writing this book through conversations, e-mail correspondence, or specific recommendations. Among them are: Tom Allen, Barbara A. Bottger, Holly Carlson, Michael Carlson, Julie Dewerth-Jaffe, Rebekah Eppley, Cynthia Fazzini, Judy Feld, Randi Griner, Emily Heath, Gary Heath, Jill James, Dodd Lamberton, Gordon Lathrop, Paul Lutter, Pam Marolla, Vince Marolla, Ellen Meissgeier, Donnita Moeller, Kathie Nycklemoe, Dale Olen, Joelyn Olen, Amy Reumann, Mary Rowland, Jane Rubietta, Steve Rye, Andrea Lee Schieber, Barb Scotty, Pam Shellberg, Robert Sitze, Cynthia Leitich Smith, Carol E. Spencer, James Stein, Lowell Timm, Vivian Thomas-Breitfeld, Kris Totzke, Jean Morris Trumbauer, Jan Veseth-Rogers, and the staff of Christos Ministries.

We thank Bishop Peter Rogness, who supported and recognized our writing as ministry and encouraged us to pursue it.

We thank the people who helped us care for our children while writing this book: Diane and Dick Mclander, Linda and Sam Eppley, the teachers of Premiere Ecole preschool, and the teachers at Milwaukee German Immersion School.

Finally, we thank God for bringing us together and giving us the desire and the ability to write (and still love each other in the morning).

Section One

Creating a Life Vision

Mining Your Childhood and Youth

You are all the ages you have ever been. Long before you became a spiritual leader you were an infant, then a child, an adolescent, and a young adult. Although long ago you may have cast aside some of your childish ways, you continue to be a child of God. Whether you remember your childhood with fondness or disappointment, your early years of life shaped the kind of person and spiritual leader you have become.

This week you will dig around in your past to make connections between your childhood and your current life situation. The purpose of this week's activities is not to delve into deep psychological analysis but simply to make connections between your childhood interests and aspirations and your current life. This week's exercises may lead you to discover long-lost passions and dreams. They may provide evidence that God was calling you to become a spiritual leader from the beginning. In any case, these exercises will serve as a first step toward understanding who you are today and how you might want to begin changing your life.

Connecting with Yourself

1. Recall some of your "favorite things" from your preadolescent years and list them in your journal. Record the first things that come to your mind. What or who was your favorite . . . activity, place, friend, hero, role model, relative, teacher, pet, toy, book, game, hobby, food, holiday, school subject, color, dream for your future, television show, movie, or song?
    - Do you detect any patterns in your preferences?
    - Did anything surprise you?

- As you review the list, what persons, activities, or things hold special appeal for you?

You may choose to repeat this exercise, focusing on your adolescent years.

2. Look through some of your childhood treasures. This might include pictures, scrapbooks, stuffed animals, books, toys, and other mementos.

    As you do this, ponder the following questions:
    - Why have you saved these particular childhood treasures?
    - What memories do you associate with these items?
    - How do these items relate to your current life?
    - What treasures that you haven't saved do you wish you still had access to?

    If you do not have many childhood treasures, you may choose instead to go to a place that was important to you as a child or find pictures of that place. What happened there? In what ways was that place significant?

3. In your journal, make a list of some of the activities, ideas, and dreams that you were passionate about as a child or teenager. Choose at least two of these and write or think about how they affected your life in the past and continue to affect your life today.

4. Make a connection with someone you knew in your childhood—a parent, grandparent, sibling, aunt, uncle, cousin, teacher, neighbor, or friend. Ask them what they remember about you as a child or teenager. Here are some questions to get you started: What was I interested in? What was I talented at? What was my personality like? What did I talk about doing when I grew up?

Connecting with a Partner

1. What did you learn from doing the exercises in Connecting with Yourself? What information did you discover that you had forgotten? What surprising things did you recall about your childhood? How do other people's memories of you as a child compare to your own memories?

2. In what ways are your childhood passions and dreams reflected in your current life and work situations?

3. Describe aspects of your childhood that are not currently part of your life. Are they still important to you? Why or why not? Which aspects

of your childhood would you like to incorporate into your current life situation? (This might include relationships, activities, or learning opportunities.)

Connecting with God

Try one or all of the following activities this week.
- Create a symbol that reflects your childhood identity. You might use a photo or one of your childhood treasures. You may also sculpt, paint, or draw a picture that captures your specific interests. Put this symbol in your place of prayer as a reminder of your childhood self.
- Use one of your childhood prayers or songs in your daily prayer time this week.
- During your prayer time, and as you go about your activities this week, picture yourself as a child being unconditionally loved by God.

Challenge

Recall an activity that you enjoyed as a child in which you do not currently participate (examples include music, playing games, camping, carpentry, sports, painting, dancing, walking in nature, gardening, astronomy, animal care, sewing, crafting). Add this activity to your routine this week. If this activity requires a partner or a team, enlist the help of your partner, a friend, or your local community league.

Week Two

Exploring Your Faith Journey

The process of becoming a spiritual leader may be compared to a journey. The traveler encounters curves and bumps along the way, ponders roads not taken, and may even wander aimlessly for awhile. You may not often take time to stop and ask, "How did I get here?" And yet, you can benefit from this endeavor. Before you can begin to consider who you are and where you might be going, it is helpful to review the path you have traveled thus far. No doubt many people, experiences, and events directed you to where you are today. This week you will take time to consider these influences and reflect on their place in your current life and ministry.

Connecting with Yourself

1. Write the following sentence beginning in your journal three times: "I am a spiritual leader because . . ." Quickly, without analysis, finish each sentence with the first idea that comes to your mind.
2. Create a life-map of your journey to becoming a spiritual leader. Beginning with your childhood and continuing through your current life and work situation, include the internal and external experiences and events that nudged you towards becoming a spiritual leader. These might include (but are not limited to) an experience you had in church or synagogue as a small child, conversations you had with others, or educational experiences. On a large piece of newsprint or tag board, draw pictures or write words that indicate each event.

    When you have finished your map, take a moment to reflect on the patterns that emerged. Do you see any points that you might have moved in a different direction? Indicate those on the map. Circle the three events that you see as being most influential in your journey to becoming a spiritual leader.

What sort of titles would you give to the various stages of your journey? Examples include: Smooth Sailing, A Long and Winding Road, Rocky Roads, The Accidental Tourist, The Path of Least Resistance.

3. Make a list of the people who have been your spiritual leaders throughout your life. What have you learned from them? What role did they play in your decision to become a spiritual leader?

Connecting with a Partner

1. Tell the story of your life-map. Talk about the most influential events and experiences and the points where you might have moved in other directions. What patterns do you observe in your partner's map?
2. How do the answers to the statements "I am a spiritual leader because . . ." relate to the discoveries you have made in drawing your life-map? Did the two exercises give you different or similar perspectives on your journey to becoming a spiritual leader?
3. In what ways do both your spiritual journey and your current ministry reflect the influence of spiritual leaders who have been your role models?

Connecting with God

Use your life-map as a part of your daily prayer time. Think about how God has been present to you in key moments in your life. Express gratitude to God for that presence in a way that is comfortable to you.

Challenge

Revisit a spiritual influence from your past journey. If possible, connect with a spiritual leader of your past. Write a letter or call to thank this person for the influence he or she has had in your life. If it is not possible to connect with a living spiritual leader, use your journal to write a thank-you note to one of your mentors.

Week Three

Discovering Your Authentic Self

One of our most agonizing memories of seminary was a class called "homiletics lab." We practiced our sermon delivery while being recorded on videotape. Then we were subjected to viewing the results while being critiqued by our merciless peers. Painful as it was, this experience allowed us to see ourselves more objectively.

Many of us find it difficult to take an honest look at our lives. A number of factors contribute to this difficulty. We may busy ourselves with external activities that allow little time for introspection. Sometimes we have trouble being honest about ourselves because who we are doesn't match up with who we think we ought to be. Some of us fear what we might find when we gaze deep inside. Others might consider extended self-reflection to be a vain, self-indulgent activity.

Self-improvement begins with self-knowledge. Biblical prophets shed the light of truth on the people who were sitting in darkness. Prophets made honest observations about the present, providing their hearers with the tools to begin to change. This week you will function as your own prophet—looking at who you are and telling the truth about what you see. These nuggets of information will form part of the foundation for the work you will do in future weeks.

Connecting with Yourself

1. Imagine that you are writing a letter to a person you have never met. Assume that this person lives in a different country and culture and knows nothing about your faith tradition. How would you describe yourself? Include your likes and dislikes, how you spend your time,

adjectives that get at the heart of your personality, what brings you meaning and joy, the events and people that are most important to you, and anything else that you identify with yourself. Write an actual letter. Do not self-edit. If you are more of a visual thinker, you may draw pictures as well.

When you have finished, read your letter.
- Which parts (if any) surprised you?
- If you were the recipient, what questions would you want to ask the writer?
- Are there parts of your life you were reticent to share?
- What areas do you cover most thoroughly?
- What does this letter tell you about who you are (and how you perceive yourself)?

2. "A picture is worth a thousand words."
    a. Find pictures of yourself in many of the roles you identify with your life. Examples include as a child, as a spouse, as a parent, as an athlete, while on vacation, and in your role as a spiritual leader (perhaps choose two, one at the beginning of your public ministry and one now).
    b. Spend some time observing each photograph and reflecting. What do you remember about the situation? What were you thinking at that time? How were you feeling? Were you energized or drained? What caused you to feel that way? Were you being yourself? Which picture represents the most authentic you?
    c. You may want to mount the pictures on tag board or in your journal and make a list of words under and around each picture describing what you felt and thought at the time the picture was taken. You may also want to write (in a different color ink) about what you think and feel about that situation today.

Connecting with a Partner

1. Show the picture you found to be "the most authentic you" and explain why you consider it to be so.
2. Sometimes another person can see us better than we can see ourselves. Visit each other's homes or offices this week. Observe the environment (making note of items such as decorations, wall hangings, mementos, books, electronic entertainment equipment, and furniture). If you did

not know your partner, what assumptions would you make about the person who lives or works in this space?

How do your observations compare with how your partner sees himself or herself?

Connecting with God

Use the picture that most represents the "authentic you" during your prayer time this week. Thank God for making you who you are. Ask God to help you let your light shine.

Meditate upon one or more of the following scripture passages during the coming week: Ps. 139:1-18; Jer. 1:5; Isa. 43:1-2; Matt. 5:14-16; or Rom. 12:1-2.

Challenge

At the end of each day reflect on your daily conversations and activities. You might want to make a list of the most significant ones in your journal. At which points during the day did you sense that you were being most authentically yourself (you spoke and acted in ways that were genuine to your personality, values, and beliefs)? Make note of the times when you felt like you were not being your authentic self. This might include times when you felt uncomfortable or awkward, your responses—laughter or speech—did not feel natural but forced, or you did not feel that you were being true to your values or beliefs as you interacted with others.

Examining the Shape of Your Daily Life

We once heard a preacher declare that one could know the condition of people's lives by peering into two books: their checkbook and their date book. How we spend our time and money indicates which relationships, ideas, and activities we value most.

What would your date book reveal about you? When you wake each day and ponder the activities laid out before you like stepping stones through the future, do you want to jump into the first activity or go back to bed? An examination of your daily routine provides an opportunity to see your life from both the outside and the inside. This week you will look at where your time really goes. (Ten hours a week watching television? Never!) You will also consider how your regular daily activities affect your energy level. At the end of the week, we hope you'll have some clues about how you would like to see your life change—for the better.

Connecting with Yourself

1. During the coming weeks, you will use your journal to keep track of how you actually spend your hours.

   Before you begin, write down how you think you spend your time. Try to give yourself numerical values; for example, "I spend six hours a night sleeping."

   Create a chart to use as a guide for keeping track of how you spend your hours. You will be doing this through week nine. You will use this information to set your priorities at work and at home.

   Use the following categories:

- Work (This includes any tasks related to your work. Remember to include commuting time, time spent working on your job tasks while at home, and time spent in social activities related to your job.)
- Daily tasks (These might include cooking, cleaning, showering, laundry, yard chores, grocery shopping, and so forth.)
- Relationships (This includes both fun and dutiful events with your family and friends. Use this space for your book group, parent-teacher conferences, and so forth.)
- Self-care (This may include sleep, exercise, reading, relaxing, entertainment, praying, and personal devotional time.)
- Other (Use this category for anything that does not fit into the other five categories.)

2. Do this exercise at the end of the week, after you have completed exercise 1.

    a. Look at all of the activities on your record of the past week. Put a plus sign next to each activity that boosts your energy. Put a minus sign next to those activities that drain you. Some will be neither—indicate that with a small circle. Some activities will have elements of each, so put both signs down.

    b. When you have finished, take two colored highlighters. In the color you like the most, highlight every item that you rated as a "plus." In the color you like the least, highlight each item that you rated as a "minus." Do not do anything with those items that have elements of each or neither.

    c. Calculate the amount of time you spend in each category: energy boosting, energy draining, and neutral.

    d. You may want to record your initial impressions about your energy boosts and drains in your journal.

This is how Pastor Simon, a recent seminary graduate who is single, began his chart:

Table 1.1

Work	Daily Tasks	Relationships	Self-Care	Other
Sermon prep 8 hours +	Yard work 2 hours +	Walking dog 3 hours +	Sleeping 42 hours +	Weekly food pantry work 1 hour +
Office hours 16 hours +/-	Garbage 15 minutes ()	Weekly sports night with friends 3 hours +	Television 10 hours +	Surfing the Internet 3 hours +
Visiting shut-ins 8 hours -	Cooking 2 hours -	Coffee Date 1 hour +	Devotional Reading 3.5 hours +	
Committee work 5 hours -	Cleaning 1 hour -	Phone call to parents 1/2 hour +	Lifting weights 2 hours +	
Preparing and Leading Bible Class 6 hours +	Laundry 2 hours -		Doctor's appointment 1 hour -	
Continued...	Continued...	Continued...	Continued...	Continued...

3. Clearly one week cannot encompass the activities you participate in, both professionally and personally, over the course of a year. Are there any additional activities (not included in your chart) that you find to be especially draining or energizing? This might include funerals, weddings, vacation Bible school, holiday festivities, vacations, educational leave, or community events. Make a list for each category.

Connecting with a Partner

1. Look together at your charts that indicate energy boosts and drains and answer the following questions.
    *   What patterns do you see in your chart? In your partner's chart?
    *   What conclusions might you draw about your partner's values and interests from this list of energy boosts and drains?

- How have these energy drains and boosts affected you as a spiritual leader?
- How do you cope with ministry tasks that drain your energy?

2. Show your chart about how you spend your time. Compare your "before chart" with the journal of your daily activities.
    - How well or poorly did you predict your activities and commitments?
    - What surprises you about how you spend your time?
    - To which areas of your life do you wish to devote more time? To which areas of your life do you wish to devote less time?

Connecting with God

Begin and end each day this week with this prayer or one like it: *Thank you, God, for the gift of this day. I offer it back as my gift to you.*

Meditate on one or more of the following scripture readings this week: Psalm 90:1-12; Psalm 118:24; or Ecclesiastes 3:1-8.

Challenge

Choose to do one of the following:

1. Select one energy drain that you can modify or eliminate from your schedule this week. Pastor Simon found cooking to be an energy drain because he waited until supper time each night to decide what he would eat. He solved this energy drain by creating a weekly menu and shopping list.
2. Select one energy boost for which you rarely have time and find a way to add it to your weekly schedule. Pastor Isabella loved to run but could only do it on her day off because of daily office hours. She modified her office hours to allow herself time to run four days a week.

Envisioning Your Ideal Life

Any creative endeavor begins with a vision. Who can imagine a cathedral being built, brick by brick, without an architect first envisioning the final product and setting down the plans? One way to consider your present life—and to begin thinking about what you might want to change—is to envision your ideal life.

Victor Frankl said, "One does not invent one's mission, one detects it." You have already taken out your magnifying glass and snooped around in your past and present. You will now take your detective skills and turn to the future—asking God to bless both the process and the product. The process that you begin this week will continue throughout the year as you consider various aspects of your life.

Connecting with Yourself

1. Review the exercises and discussions about your authentic self from week three. What clues does this information give you about your ideal life? Make a list in your journal. For example, if someone feels most authentically herself when she is with people who share her commitments to social justice, her ideal life might include working or living with people committed to justice issues.

2. Look at the records you have been making of your daily activities since week four. What are the aspects of your current life situation that you would want to incorporate into your ideal life?

3. Whose life and values do you admire? Why? Use one or more of the following techniques to explore this person's life further. You may do this exercise more than once.

- Interview this person.
- Write an imaginary dialogue with him or her.
- Read this person's work, talk to his or her colleagues, explore how he or she arrived at an ideal life.

4. Imagine your "ideal life." Use the clues you unearthed in the first three exercises to guide you. Dream big. Consider what you would do if you were not restricted by money, time, and training. This "big dream" will give you clues about your current life and the direction that you need to journey in the future.

    a. The visual alternative. Make a collage (using magazines, your own pictures, buttons, beads, ribbons, and anything else you want) of your ideal life. Don't think too much—simply cut the pictures and words that attract you and arrange and attach them on a large piece of tag board. You may choose to address where you would like to live, what you would like to be doing, and how and with whom you would spend your time.

    b. The verbal alternative. Describe your vision of your ideal life in your journal. Record the ideas that come to you without judgment or censure. You may wish to address the following questions:
        - Where do you live?
        - With whom do you live?
        - What do your days look like?
        - What is your work?
        - What are your hobbies?

Connecting with a Partner

1. Discuss the process of imagining your ideal life. With what in this process did you struggle? What about this process came easily to you?
2. Share your description of your ideal life. What themes do you see emerging from your own and your partner's ideal life portraits? How does this vision of your ideal life relate to your current ministry situation?
3. Your vision is the first step towards setting down a plan to change your life. Discuss how you might make your vision a reality using the following questions:
    - Do you think your vision is attainable? Why or why not?
    - What steps would it take to get from here to there?
    - What would be appropriate first steps toward reaching your vision?

Connecting with God

Someone once said that God can dream a bigger dream for us than we can dream for ourselves. Keeping that in mind, begin and end each day with this prayer or one like it: *God of my future, show me the vision toward which you are leading me.*

Challenge

Spend at least two hours this week exploring one of the aspects of your ideal life that intrigues you.

Pastor Amy always wanted to live in the mountains. She looked at photographic books about the mountains, researched places of interest on the Internet, and took a long walk in a state park, imagining what it might be like to live in the mountains. Jose, a church musician, dreamed of going to graduate school. He spent a morning leafing through graduate school guides at his local library and then visited a nearby college for lunch, pondering how he would feel about being a student again.

Linda, a parish administrator, envisioned her church starting a literacy program for children. She spent the afternoon at her local bookstore, envisioning ways that she could share her love of books with children. That evening, she ate dinner with the director of a local literacy center and observed the evening program.

Overcoming Obstacles

You may have a voice inside your head that is shouting, "This book is a waste of time! I cannot change my life. Why imagine the impossible?" Like an architect, you may know how to dream up a cathedral and even draft the plans. Even so, you may argue, you lack the money and resources to put your plans into action.

This week you will face the forces within and around you that may keep you mired in your current situation, no matter how unpleasant that situation may be. All of us experience some fear about changing our lives and receive some benefit from keeping them the way they are. One temptation might be to banish those fears and simply not deal with them. Another is to let them take over—and stop the process of change. We think it is best to meet our fears and other obstacles face to face. This week you will treat your fears and excuses as if they are people. You will listen to them and, with God's help, respond to what they are saying.

Connecting with Yourself

1. In your journal, make a chart with two columns. On the left side, make a list of all of the reasons that you think you will never be able to change your life or achieve your ideal life. Include the reasons you might hear from colleagues, family, friends, and people in your ministry setting. On the right side, write a refutation to each argument (even if you don't yet believe it!). Father Carlos, who dreamed about getting a doctor of ministry degree, wrote:

Table 1.2

I don't have enough money.	I can save for a year and then go.
I'm too old.	Plenty of people my age are doing continuing education.
There isn't a program in my area.	I could check out distance learning options and summer courses.

2. All of us receive some benefit or payoff from staying in our current life situation. In this exercise, you will consider the payoffs and costs of making choices.

   a. Think about a time when you chose not to do something you really wanted to do. What payoff did you receive from making the choice you did? What did it cost you?

      Create two columns and make two lists—one for payoffs and one for costs (you can have multiple payoffs and costs). For example, "I chose not to play on the college football team, even though I wanted to, in order to please my father, who feared it might distract me from my studies." This person's payoff was maintaining his father's approval. It cost him the opportunity to use his athletic abilities and be part of a team.

   b. Think about your present situation and some of your hopes and dreams. What payoffs would you receive by not making changes? What will it cost you?

      Again, set up two columns and make two lists. You can look at as many areas of your life as you want—career, relationships, health, and so forth. (An example might be, "The benefit of not dieting is that I can continue to eat donuts and cheeseburgers." "The cost is that these foods may contribute to health problems, and eventually shorten my life span.")

3. In your ongoing struggle against obstacles, it is helpful to distinguish between what you can and cannot control in your life. Sometimes recognizing what you can control—your attitude, for example—helps you to feel less stressed about what you cannot control.

Choose an activity that is a regular part of your life and that regularly contains obstacles that might irritate or annoy you. (For example, you might choose driving your car, shopping, attending a committee meeting, or feeding vegetables to your children.) As you experience an obstacle, ask,

- "In this situation what do I control?
- What do others control?
- What does God control?"

Let go of taking responsibility for those actions that you do not control. How does that feel to you? How might refusing to take responsibility for actions you do not control change your life?

Connecting with a Partner

1. Discuss your experience in completing exercise 3 from Connecting with Yourself.
2. In the past, how have you typically dealt with obstacles? How successful have you been? What resources have helped you?
3. Where would you place yourself on the following continuum? Why?

Illustration 1.1

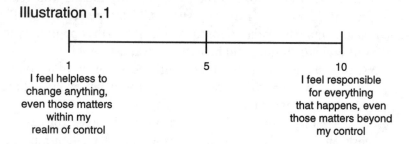

```
 1                      5                      10
I feel helpless to                    I feel responsible
change anything,                        for everything
even those matters                   that happens, even
within my                          those matters beyond
realm of control                         my control
```

- In what types of situations do you feel most in control? In which do you feel the most helpless?
- How do your feelings about control affect and reflect your relationship with God?

4. What obstacles do you anticipate continually battling as you work to improve your life? Make a list of resources you have to support you. Discuss how you can support one another during this process.

Connecting with God

Meditate each morning and evening on Jesus' saying, "For mortals it is impossible, but not for God; for God all things are possible" (Mark 10:27). Consider how your life might be different if you trusted in God's promise of abundant possibilities.

Challenge

Our language both shapes and reflects our attitudes. We can often detect our unspoken fears when we pay attention to our use of the word *but*. The word *but* stands like a giant stop sign in the midst of our sentences. It reminds us to stop and consider the critics in our lives and minds. During the next week, try to eliminate the word *but* from your speaking (and thinking). Don't forget to look at your weekly sermon or talk! (You might find it helpful—and interesting—to use the word *and* in place of the word *but*.) You may also want to listen for how others use the word but in their language.

Reflect on what you notice about your use of language, especially the word *but*. What does it say about your attitudes toward change and possibility?

Week Seven

Principles, Gifts, and Passions

Pastor Bonnie kept an "eschatological interest list" in the back of her journal. The list contained all the activities she wanted to accomplish before she died—run a marathon, swim with the dolphins, write an article for a theological journal, learn to bake pies, and so forth. Day after day of her life passed by and Pastor Bonnie never found time for any of these activities, not even for a half hour of exercise.

Pastor Bonnie is not so different from most of us. We may have a variety of passions and dreams, but our daily activities prevent us from having the time and energy to pursue our passions. Sometimes we have so many dreams for our lives that we rarely accomplish even a few of them. We benefit from making priorities and focusing on one or two at a time. One way to begin thinking about setting priorities (next week's task) is to examine the principles that guide your life, the gifts God has given you, and the passions you hold within you.

Connecting with Yourself

As you complete the following exercises, look at both your ministry and your personal life when you choose your principles, gifts, and passions. Be careful not to "take on" the principles, gifts, and passions of the institution you currently serve unless they truly are your own as well.

1. Think of a time when you did something that made you feel great while you were doing it. You felt connected to the project or activity, to God, to yourself, and to the world. Your pleasure was not about external rewards or products but about enjoying the process. Reflect in your

journal on the following questions. (This activity may provide clues as you consider your principles, gifts, and passions.)

- What were you doing?
- Who were you with?
- How did you feel connected to God in the process of what you were doing?
- Is this activity something that you do regularly or was it a once in a lifetime event?

2. A principle is a foundational law or truth. Often, a society holds certain principles to be universally true for all members. For example, the United States Declaration of Independence asserts that all people are created equal. Many religious faiths believe that forgiveness is a key principle. Still, despite universal approval for such principles, each person and group provides different definitions and gives unique weight to the same principles.

   What principles do you value? Make a list and then circle the two or three that are most important to you. Examples include: forgiveness, commitment, respect, justice, mercy, hospitality, gratitude, trust in God, integrity, honesty, human dignity, service, patience, compassion, freedom, wisdom, peace, beauty, encouragement, unity, joy, love, learning, perseverance, wholeness, grace, mindfulness, achievement, independence, security.

3. What are you gifted at? Make a list of your talents. Examples might include cooking, athletics, speaking, carpentry, welcoming others, encouraging others, knowledge in a specific field (such as nature, baseball, or quilting), and organizing. When you have completed your list, circle the two or three talents that are most essential to your life.

4. What are you passionate about? Make a list of the ideas, activities, people, and things that stir your passion. This could include music, gardening, home repair, books, movies, raising children, community activism, athletic experiences, traveling, and politics.

   When your list is complete, circle the two or three passions that you value most. If you are having trouble answering this question (or if you are having trouble answering this question without saying, "Well, I should be passionate about _____"), consider these questions:

- What would you do if you had no constraints such as time or money?
- What do you fantasize about that you are hesitant to share with others?
- What would you regret not doing if you died today?

5.   Compile your most valued principles, gifts, and passions on an index card. You will be using this list with your partner.

Connecting with a Partner

1.   Discuss your choices of principles, gifts, and passions. How are you currently making use of these in your life? In what ways do you see yourself making more use of them in the future?
2.   There are many expectations about what a spiritual leader should be passionate about. To what extent do the principles, gifts, and passions you chose reflect the expectations of your calling as a spiritual leader, your ministry setting, or your colleagues?
3.   What was the experience of narrowing your lists down to two or three items like for you? What do you think this says about your ability to focus or select priorities?

Connecting with God

Select an item that relates to one of your principles, gifts, or passions. Use it during your prayer time each day this week, creating a prayer that connects the object to your faith. Pastor Kristi recently rediscovered her gift for crochet. She chose an afghan crocheted by her grandmother and prayed, "Cover me with your love, gracious God." Father Nick loved baseball and chose his baseball glove. Each day he prayed, "Remind me that you hold me in your hands, dear God." If you cannot think of a prayer, you might choose to use this one: *Creator, work through my gifts to lead me to you.*

Challenge

Watch a movie by which you remember being inspired when you saw it the first time. How does this film connect to your current principles, gifts, and passions?

Setting and Keeping Priorities

"My family is my top priority," proclaims Pastor Joe. Most everyone believes him. Sometimes, however, his wife and children have doubts—like when he insists on answering the telephone during the family supper hour and talking with a parishioner for 20 minutes about altar flowers while the food gets cold.

In your multi-tasked life as a spiritual leader, you can easily lose sight of your priorities. Despite a strong sense of your principles, gifts, and passions, your time and energies may be drained by the demands of the moment. By being intentional about your priorities, you can shape more of your life than you might believe is possible.

Because time and energy are limited, when you say yes to something you are always saying no to something else. You have priorities, whether you intentionally choose them or not. Your priorities are not what you say is most important or even what you think is most important—they are what you do with the time you have each day. This week you will use the work you did last week to discern the priorities by which you want to live.

Connecting with Yourself

1. Review the daily activity lists you have been keeping since week four, paying specific attention to the nonwork-related items. Note the amount of time you spend working, though not necessarily what work tasks get the most of your time (you will look at that next week). On the basis of these lists, decide which activities you are currently giving priority to. Then review the list of your principles, gifts, and passions from week seven.

Make a "priority list" of the five items that are most important to you. This list will function as an activity screen for you. Each request you receive and each idea you have can be filtered through this list. Ask yourself, "Is this on my priority list?" If it isn't, ask, "Does this fit into my life or can it be turned down?" (In the next section on work, you will consider the role of "emergencies" in the spiritual leader's life and how that fits into your priority list. For now, know that real emergencies still take priority.)

After each item on your priority list, list one or two specific ways that you hope to nurture this priority. The list is not simply a way of cutting out the things that do not fit into your life, but of adding value and richness to the items on your list. Keep the list simple. Do not overload yourself with many demands. In the next section you will have the opportunity to create a list of your priorities for your work life.

Jennifer is a pastor of a small rural congregation, married, and the mother of two school-aged children. Her example follows:

Principles: Beauty, service, trust in God
Gifts: Music, hospitality
Passions: Caring for children, cooking for others, singing
Priority List:
   a.   Take time daily to care for my spiritual self (prayer, nature walks, music).
   b.   Nurture my relationship with my husband (weekly dates, daily conversation).
   c.   Nurture my relationship with my children (daily family meals, game night).
   d.   Share my musical talents (sing with the community church choir once a week).
   e.   Serve my congregation.

2.   In this exercise you will write a theme statement for the coming year. Take time to review the exercises you have completed in the past seven weeks—your history, your present situation, your visions, your lists of principles, gifts and passions, and finally your priorities. What phrase best indicates who you are and who you want to become in this process? Examples of theme statements include: *I will let my light shine; Life is my joyful dance; Rooted in God, I am blooming; Step by step, my journey moves forward.*

Use paint, colorful markers, or a computer word processing program to make copies of your theme statement. Post these in places where you will see them often. Sometimes it helps to create a visual reinforcement to accompany your theme statement. The person who chose the statement, "Rooted in God, I am blooming" used pictures of flowers cut from magazines to illustrate her theme statement posters.

3. When embarking on a new journey in life, it is helpful to have multiple sources of support and reinforcement. A theme song can be one such source. Politicians, sports teams, and businesses understand the value of auditory reinforcement (remember Bill Clinton's "Don't Stop Thinking about Tomorrow"?).

Choose a theme song for this year. Make a recording of it and listen to it regularly—even daily. Type up the lyrics and keep a copy in your date book.

Connecting with a Partner

1. Share your theme statement and priority list.
   What challenges do you anticipate as you seek to follow this list?
2. When you begin to say no, you might feel guilty (and others may feel disappointed in you). Think about times in the past when you have said no to a request.
   - How guilty do you usually feel saying no to others?
   - How difficult do you find the process of saying no?
   - What kinds of requests do you find most difficult to turn down?
   - Are there certain people whom you find difficult to turn down?
3. Discuss a strategy for saying no to other people. You may want to try these role-plays.
   a. A member of your church invites you to a family party. You have attended these occasions in the past. This time, it falls on the same night as your weekly "family/friend fun night." You kindly say no. The parishioner responds, "But we really wanted you to say the blessing. Besides, a lot of the parish will be coming, too." How do you respond?
   b. A member of the community interfaith commission invites you to chair the committee to create a community food pantry. Your church responsibilities are currently quite heavy and your priorities do not

allow the time for you to do this. You politely decline. The member says, "But the committee will never be successful unless we have you as the chair or at least as a member." How do you respond?

Connecting with God

Find scripture passages that reinforce your theme statement. Write these down with your theme statement on an index card and keep them with your devotional materials. Daily, ask God to guide you as you aspire to maintain your priorities.

Challenge

One way to keep to your priority list is to never make an immediate decision. When someone asks you something that requires a commitment on your part, answer, "I'll have to think about that and get back to you tomorrow."

Make a commitment this week to use this statement to respond to every request that doesn't fit with your priority list. At the end of the week, talk with your partner about how it went.

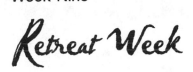

Retreat Week

This retreat week is designed to give you another opportunity and setting from which to consider your life's vision. Refer to the introduction for a description of the purpose and structure of a retreat week. As you create a retreat that is nurturing for you, you may want to use some of the following movies, books, and activities.

MOVIES AND VIDEO

City Slickers
Three Manhattan buddies sign up for a western cattle drive and learn a lesson about accomplishing goals.

Cold Comfort Farm
Orphaned Flora Poste stays with rural relatives and coaches them to follow their life's vision.

The Contender
A woman, chosen to succeed a deceased vice president, adheres to her principles despite public embarrassments during the approval process.

Jerry Maguire
Maguire, a sports agent, writes a mission statement that changes everything.

Shirley Valentine
A London housewife leaves her family for a vacation on a Greek island and in the process falls in love with herself.

BOOKS

Fiction

Catherine, Called Birdy by Karen Cushman
In this comical young adult novel set in the Middle Ages, Catherine learns to appreciate being herself.

The Education of Harriet Hatfield by May Sarton
After the death of her long-time partner, Harriet opens a feminist bookstore. In the process she comes to terms with her life's circumstances.

Frederick by Leo Lionni
In this children's picture book, Frederick the mouse learns that the gift he offers is valuable to the community.

Glittering Images by Susan Howatch
Anglican priest Charles Ashworth confronts himself and his own doubts in this fast-paced novel set in the Church of England.

Handling Sin by Michael Malone
Raleigh Whittier Hayes embarks on a journey to rescue his father and ultimately reconnects with both God and himself.

Miss Rumphius by Barbara Cooney
In this beautifully illustrated book for children, Miss Rumphius meets her father's challenge: to make the world a more beautiful place.

The Mixed-Up Chameleon by Eric Carle
A discontent chameleon wishes to be like many of the animals in the zoo in this classic book for young children.

My Name Is Asher Lev and *The Gift of Asher Lev* by Chaim Potok
Asher Lev confronts many obstacles as he pursues his God-given gift of painting.

The Pull of the Moon by Elizabeth Berg
A woman journeys to new venues and in the process learns to appreciate what she has at home.

A Wrinkle in Time by Madeleine L'Engle
In this children's novel, Meg, Calvin, and Charles set out on an adventure to rescue Meg and Charles's father. On the journey, Meg learns that she has all that she needs within herself.

Nonfiction

Let Your Life Speak: Listening for the Voice of Vocation by Parker J. Palmer
In this series of essays, Palmer challenges readers to be faithful to their inner voice.

Living Your Best Life by Laura Berman Fortgang.
Fortgang offers a three-step process for achieving one's life vision.

Smart Choices: Making Your Way through Life by Rochelle Melander and Harold Eppley
This small group guide directs you through the process of writing a personal mission statement.

Take Time for Your Life by Cheryl Richardson
Coach Cheryl Richardson presents a process to help readers make better life-choices.

Tuesdays with Morrie by Mitch Album
Album's account of his professor's last months contains many insights about living and dying.

An Unknown Woman by Alice Koller
In this memoir, Koller goes alone to the coast for a retreat to discover who she is and what she is meant to do.

What Are You Doing with the Rest of Your Life? Choices in Mid-Life by Paula Payne Hardin
This book considers mid-life changes and provides keys for living a generative life at any age.

ACTIVITIES

This might be a good time to explore some of the challenges that you did not have time to complete during the previous eight weeks. You may also want to repeat a challenge that was particularly useful to you. The following weekly challenges are best suited to a retreat: weeks one, two, five, and seven.

- Write a letter to yourself or a close friend, dated one year from today. Write about how your life has changed in the past year. What have you accomplished? In what ways have you moved closer to living your ideal life? Use present tense and include many details. When you are finished, you may choose to seal this letter and open it a year from now. If you prefer, you may use the letter as a guide for making choices in the coming year.
- Spend time visualizing yourself living your ideal life.
- Choose a biblical character whose life vision inspires you. Read about that character in scripture and other sources. Ponder what you can learn from this person's experience.
- Visit an art museum or gallery either in person or online and allow yourself to be inspired by the creative vision of the artist.
- Explore a great work of architecture. Imagine the steps that were taken to create this work from conception to completion.
- Ask a spiritual director or a friend (other than your discussion partner) to listen as you talk about your life vision.
- Do one or more Internet searches related to key aspects of your life vision.
- Select and review magazines related to your life vision from your local library or bookstore.
- For fun, visit www.cmi-lmi.com/kingdomality.html to discover your medieval vocational personality.
- Visit www.emode.com for more personality tests, such as what kind of dog you would be.

Section Two

Caring for Yourself at Work

Setting Priorities at Work

Over the years, we've kept a list of those ministry tasks we never learned how to do at seminary. We expect some day to present them to our former professors, maybe even teach a class about them to new clergy. Here are a few of them: fix a copy machine; make 100 cups of coffee; stand on a folding chair and change the eternal flame; turn palms into ashes; negotiate with the United States Post Office when your bulk mailing does not meet current standards; or fix a bride's torn train in five minutes or less.

You get the picture. Much of what you do in a week does not fit into your job description or even remotely relate to your call as a spiritual leader. Besides the regular duties outlined in your job description (if you have one), you must deal with the individual expectations of members, colleagues, and community leaders. Each day you juggle your regular duties, the stuff on your agenda, and the emergencies that arise. Like the best-laid plans of mice, spiritual leaders' plans often go awry!

Within this reality, setting priorities is vital. As you discovered in week eight, even people who do not set priorities end up making choices about what's most important. Unfortunately, they often choose what is immediate over what is essential. This week you will think about how these issues apply to your working life.

Connecting with Yourself

1. In this exercise you will sift through all of the tasks you do and are asked to do for the purpose of discerning your ministry priorities.

   On a large sheet of paper, list everything you do during the course of a year that is related to your role as a spiritual leader. Include those tasks that you may do on occasion even though they are not directly ministry related (examples include turning on the heat in the sanctuary before services, mowing the church lawn, and baking for the Sunday school bake sale).

Circle your five most important ministry tasks. These tasks will generally be items that rely on your training and your call to this ministry. Include tasks that affect the most people, tasks that are included in your job description, and tasks that you consider to be vital to your ministry.

Copy this list of ministry priorities and post it in your date book and in a prominent place in your office. If you use computers, consider putting this list on your screensaver or in your handheld.

2. For many spiritual leaders, the problem isn't determining priorities—it is getting to them. In this exercise you will begin to work on eliminating some of the unnecessary tasks that prevent you from focusing on your priorities.

In your journal, create a grid with four boxes. Down the left side, label the rows "priority" and "nonpriority." Across the top, write above the first column "to be done by me," and above the second "to be done by others."

This produces four categories:
- Priority, to be done by me (for example, sermon preparation).
- Nonpriority, to be done by me (an example might include reviewing resources for the church library).
- Priority, to be done by someone else (an example might include choosing music for Sunday worship).
- Nonpriority, to be done by someone else (an example might include cleaning and arranging craft supplies for Sunday school).

Using your list from the previous exercise, record your priority list under "priority, to be done by me." Assign the items not circled in exercise 1 to the remaining categories. Save this list for the work you will do with your partner and for next week.

Connecting with a Partner

1. In the past, what choices have you made that prevented you from being faithful to your priorities?
2. What do you foresee being the biggest challenge in keeping your priorities?
3. Look at your grid from exercise 2 in Connecting with Yourself. Brainstorm ways that each of you can eliminate, delegate, or share tasks that can be done by someone else. Begin to create plans for doing so.

   You may want to identify a committee, such as the staff support committee, to help you with this task. You may want to approach a committee related to the task, and ask them for help. For example, you could talk with the worship committee about relieving you of the task of choosing music for Sunday worship. You can also make a list of individuals who could take on some of these tasks.

Connecting with God

Reflect on how the messages of the following scripture passages speak to your task of setting and keeping ministry priorities: Exod. 18:13-27 and Acts 6:1-7.

Pray with your work priority list before you every day and ask God to help you keep your priorities in order.

Challenge

Choose one of the tasks that you currently do that you could delegate and ask someone else to take on the responsibility.

Working More Effectively

His parishioners call him "the rambling Rev." Each week Pastor Charles's sermons extend way past everyone's attention span. Pastor Charles struggles to find a morning—when his mind is most clear—to write his sermon, despite the fact that he considers this one of his most important tasks. Regularly, he does not sit down to begin his sermon preparation until Saturday evening and at least once a month, he decides to "wing it."

Pastor Charles is not the only spiritual leader who has difficulty working effectively. We all must squeeze myriad tasks into a limited number of hours. Setting priorities, as you did last week, helps to put in our minds what we "should" be focusing on each day. This week you will work on exercises that will help you to discern where you are putting your energy and time and what tasks you do best at various times of day. Hopefully these exercises will lead you to a more effective work schedule—so that you can make the best use of the limited number of hours you have.

Connecting with Yourself

1. Look at your grid from Connecting with Yourself, exercise 2 in week nine.

    Next to each activity, identify the average amount of time per week that you need to do each task effectively. You may want to review the time records you have been keeping since week four to get an actual record of the time you spend on each task. If any of your ministry tasks are events that take place once a year (such as the stewardship campaign or small-group ministry kickoff), mark down two numbers—

the time it takes you in an average week and the time it takes you during the months you are highly focused on the event's preparation and execution.

Are your priorities getting enough of your time? Are you spending too much time on tasks that are not most important to your ministry?

2. One way to maximize one's time is to do tasks at the time of day when one can most easily accomplish them. For example, an introvert's sermon might go faster when written early in the morning, when all is quiet. For extroverts, who gain energy in their time with people, writing might best be done in the afternoon, after a busy morning of visiting.

Divide a piece of paper into three columns. In the left column, write the following time slots: 6–9 A.M.; 9 A.M.–12 P.M.; 12–3 P.M.; 3–6 P.M.; 6–9 P.M.; 9 P.M.–12 A.M.

In the second column, write "physical tasks; mental tasks; social tasks," next to each time slot. Next to each type of task rank on a scale of 1 to 5 (1 = low energy; 5 = high energy) the amount of energy you generally have for that type of task during that time slot.

Finally, in the third column, note what you generally do during those hours in a typical week. An example follows.

Table 2.1

6–9 A.M.	physical: 1	sleep, quiet spiritual time, breakfast and coffee
	mental: 3	
	social: 1	
9 A.M.–12 A.M.	physical: 4	study, sermon and teaching preparation,
	mental: 5	phone calls
	social: 3	

When you have completed this task, consider the following questions:

- Looking at both your schedule and this chart, are you doing tasks at the time of day that is most effective for you?
- Are you clustering activities (doing similar types of activities at one time)? For example, do you return all your phone calls during the same time period?
- Is it possible for you to rearrange your schedule so that you can perform most of your specific tasks at the time of day that you are most energized to do them and to cluster similar types of activities?
- What would your schedule look like if you did this? Create for yourself an "ideal" schedule that reflects these changes.

Note that some aspects of your schedule, such as worship services, cannot be changed to fit your ideal schedule. If you work with a staff, or even a secretary and volunteers, the schedules of several people might have to be considered for changes to be made. It might be helpful to have your entire staff do these exercises and consider meeting times based on everyone's working style.

Connecting with a Partner

1. What insights have you gained about how you spend your time at work?
2. In what ways might knowing about your peak energy periods help you to organize your time?
3. How close are you to living by your ideal schedule?
4. What obstacles stand in the way of your being able to work more effectively?

Connecting with God

Reflect on Eccles. 3:1-8. How have these words been true in your life and the lives of those you care about? How do these words help you each day as you sort out your various tasks?

Incorporate the words from Ps. 31:14-15a into your prayers: "But I trust in you, O LORD; I say 'You are my God.' My times are in your hand."

Sing the hymn, "O God, Our Help in Ages Past."

Challenge

Take your "ideal" schedule and try to incorporate as much of it as possible into your real life. Keeping in mind that some aspects of your schedule cannot be changed or may intersect with other people's schedules, focus first on those things you can change without needing to negotiate with others.

Handling Urgencies and Emergencies

Jesus' exhortation to "be ready" (Matt. 24:44) might well be read at every pastor's ordination service. The ministry requires a "24/7" mentality, a readiness to cope with emergencies at any moment. Some spiritual leaders may feel like they are hooked up to the receiving end of 911.

An emergency is any situation that is sudden, serious, and requires your immediate attention. In a true emergency, giving immediate pastoral care or attention is the most helpful way to deal with the situation and delay might actually cause harm. When the church kitchen is on fire, it requires water—immediately. When a parishioner's child has been injured in an accident, the family requires immediate attention.

One of the toughest aspects of ministry is discerning both true emergencies and truly urgent matters. Many spiritual leaders leave a message on the answering machine at their ministry setting, "In case of an emergency, call me at home." The calls we have received range from true emergencies to queries about church service times, opening doors, and bus money. For the caller, no doubt, the question felt truly urgent. This week, you will have the opportunity to define your own criteria for discerning true "urgencies and emergencies." In doing this, you will gain more control over your time and be better able to keep your priorities.

Connecting with Yourself

1. Divide a sheet in your journal into three columns, making the center column the largest. Leave room at the top for column headings. In the center column, list those situations in the last year of your ministry in which people have demanded or requested your immediate attention.

When you have completed the list, add title headings for each of the three columns. They should read, from left to right: "actual emergency," "situation," and "I responded as though it was an emergency."

Review the list. In the left-hand column, star each item that fits the definition of an actual emergency—a situation that requires immediate attention to prevent further harm. In the right-hand column, star each item that you responded to as though it were an emergency. An example follows.

Table 2.2

Actual Emergency	Situation	I responded as though it was an emergency
	unlock the church door	*
*	Mr. Maki's car accident	*
*	pregnant teenager needs help	*
	wrong name in printed wedding bulletin	*

Reflect on the following questions in your journal:

- As you look at your list, do you see yourself as an overresponder or an underresponder?
- If you tend to be an underresponder (you do not respond immediately to emergencies), how has that affected your life and ministry?
- If you tend to be an overresponder (you respond to nonemergency situations as emergencies), how does that impact your life and ministry?

2.   Your weekly tasks tend to fall into four categories:

Table 2.3

Immediate Priorites	Nonimmediate Priorities
Tasks that are before you at the moment which require your direct attention. Almost always, these tasks must be attended to in a timely fashion. Examples include emergencies and project deadlines.	Tasks that are not immediately in front of you but that you or your congregation have designated as priorities. Generally these tasks can be overlooked for a while, but neglecting them will have definite negative consequences. These tasks might includes visits, sermon preparation, evangelism work, or youth work.
Immediate Nonpriorities	Nonimmediate Nonpriorities
Tasks that are before you at the moment which do not require your direct attention. These tasks, despite their immediacy, can be delayed and dealt with at a different time without negative consequences. Examples might include phone calls, mail, some requests, and some interruptions.	Tasks that are not immediately in front of you and that do not figure as priorities—but need to be done from time to time. They include responding to some of your mail, reviewing records, or returning some calls.

For the next two or three days, think about your tasks and how they fall into these categories. Notice how you naturally categorize your tasks into these four categories. Consider if and when you are allowing immediate nonpriorities to prevent you from attending to immediate or nonimmediate priorities. For example, are you answering the telephone (immediate but not necessarily urgent) while writing your sermon? What nonurgent immediate tasks are you most tempted to allow to take priority over your planned schedule?

Connecting with a Partner

1. What types of requests or requesting individuals are you more prone to respond to? What factors figure into your decisions about to what or to whom you will respond? How does the anxiety level of the requester influence your actions in any given situation?
2. For each of the following situations, discuss these two questions:
    -   How would you respond to the situation?
    -   What criteria would you use to come to that decision?
    a. It is Friday morning and you are working on Sunday's sermon in your office. The secretary announces that the head of the women's Bible study group has unexpectedly dropped by to discuss next year's Bible study book.
    b. In the midst of a deep, pastoral conversation at the home of a congregant, your cell phone rings.
    c. You have set aside the afternoon to plan your stewardship event for next month. When you get to your office, the mail contains a packet of information from a colleague who serves with you on a community task force. The note reads: "Could you review this material and get back to me with your changes ASAP?"
3. Work together on developing lists of criteria for defining urgencies and emergencies in your ministry.
4. What conversations do you need to have about this topic with others in your ministry setting?

Connecting with God

In the next week, each time that your work is interrupted by anything—a phone call, page, or knock at the door—silently pray, *Guide and bless my choices, O God.*

Challenge

One of the biggest time wasters for spiritual leaders is responding immediately to the many nonemergency interruptions that they receive each day. These interruptions can waste away your days and prevent you from getting to the ministry tasks you have deemed as priorities.

In order to clean up your schedule, identify and postpone responding to three nonemergency interruptions this week (those that fit the category of immediate nonpriorities). Develop a plan or a system to help you do this every week. For example, caller identification and a good answering system might allow you to judge whether a call is an emergency or a nonemergency.

Taking Time for Yourself

It might be argued that the commandment most broken by spiritual leaders is, "Remember the Sabbath day, and keep it holy" (Exod. 20:8). Many spiritual leaders have trouble taking their weekly day off. Reasons abound. Some spiritual leaders believe they have too much work to do to take time out. Others find it difficult to say no to requests or activities that happen to land on their day off. Some people might make requests without even realizing they are cutting into their spiritual leader's sacred time.

A bit like nightshift workers, spiritual leaders tend to put in their longest hours during the times that the people they serve are at rest (the weekend and holidays) and take their own sabbath when much of the rest of the world goes back to work. Despite the many reasons for ignoring one's sabbath time, the long-term toll on both spiritual leaders and the people they serve can be devastating. Failing to take time off can lead to impaired productivity, codependency, addictive behavior, and eventually burnout. But it doesn't have to be this way!

Just as good fences make good neighbors, healthy boundaries around your sabbath time can enhance your ministry and the work you do. This week you will explore ways to balance your work with daily, weekly, and yearly time off.

Connecting with Yourself

1. Spiritual leaders define sabbath time in a variety of ways. Most leaders lean toward cheating themselves of time they both deserve and need. The following checklist reflects a vision of the leader who has an ideal relationship with his or her sabbath time. Check each statement that is true for you.

_____ I always take off one day each week.

_____ I try to take off two consecutive days a week.

_____ I always take all of my vacation time each year.

_____ I do not return from the midst of vacation to work.

_____ I do not call in while on vacation.

_____ I take all of my study leave each year.

_____ I am planning for a sabbatical.

_____ I screen phone calls (cell and home), pages, and e-mails on my day off.

_____ I politely decline nonemergency work invitations for my day off, reminding colleagues and parishioners that it is my sabbath time.

_____ I have advocates in my ministry setting and colleagues who support and encourage me to take time off.

_____ During time off, I am able to refrain from thinking about my work.

_____ During time off, I seek to be nurtured spiritually as well as physically.

_____ When I cannot take a day off due to an emergency, I take a compensation day off.

_____ I regularly take compensation days for the holidays I work (examples include Christmas, Easter, and Memorial Day).

_____ I take time off each day for myself and for my family or significant others.

_____ I take a spiritual retreat each year.

How did you rate?

   0–5 Make sure your health insurance is up-to-date!
  6–10 You have room for improvement!
11–15 You are getting there!
   16 You did it!

2. For each item in the checklist from exercise 1, complete both of these statements in your journal:
    a. The benefits I receive when I am able to answer this question yes are . . .
    b. The costs to me when I answer this question no are . . .

3. For each statement that you did not check in exercise 1, identify the steps you would need to take to make that statement true.

Connecting with a Partner

1. What are some of the helpful behaviors you model when you take your time off?
2. Make a list of some of the reasons you find it difficult to take time off. These might include your personal and cultural attitudes toward work and rest, your congregation's history with spiritual leaders taking time off, the emotional health of the people in your ministry setting, and the cultural attitudes of the community you live in. Strategize about how you can overcome each of these issues.
3. What strategies could you use to leave your work at work so that you can be present to yourself, your family, and your friends in your time off?
4. Who supports you or could support you in taking time off? Work together at deciding the best ways of approaching these people for their support.

Connecting with God

Begin your "daily time off" (whether it is one hour or four) this week by reading one of the following passages: Gen. 2:2-3; Matt. 11:28-30; or Mark 6:30-31. Ask God to refresh your spirit in the time that you spend away from work.

Challenge

With the goal of eventually achieving a perfect score of 16, take steps to improve your score on the checklist from exercise 1 of Connecting with Yourself by at least one point this week. Do the easiest steps first!

Working with Boundaries

Like politicians and celebrities, spiritual leaders may feel as if they live in glass houses. Many pastors can tell stories about parishioners peering into the parsonage window, hoping to catch a glimpse of the true person behind the robes.

The nature of your calling as a spiritual leader includes conducting your personal life in a way that serves as a public witness to your faith. Like it or not, your actions will be scrutinized by those who know your role. If you rent an X-rated video or engage in drunken behavior in public, chances are someone will notice and comment—to you or to others. Because of this reality, those who live in glass houses need places where they can shut the door to outsiders. This week you will discover and define those "closed-door" places in your life as you consider appropriate boundaries for your personal and working space, time, and relationships.

Connecting with Yourself

1. Make a list of times in your ministry when your boundaries may have been violated by others. These incidents might include inappropriate questions or comments and violations of your physical self, home, or working space.

    For each incident reflect on these questions:
    * How did you respond?
    * What were you thinking and feeling at the time?
    * In what ways did this incident affect your ministry with the person or persons involved?

- How did this incident impact your ministry in general?
- If this incident were to happen today, how would you respond?

2. In this exercise you will define what you consider to be sacred or set apart in each of your relationships, including your relationship with yourself.

    On a large piece of newsprint, draw concentric circles—much like a dartboard. (See Illustration 2.1.) Label the circles from the inside out: self, spouse, children, extended family, friends, colleagues, and the people I serve. For each circle, write down the information, experiences, and spaces that you consider sacred to that circle. You will likely need to consult the persons in each "sacred circle" to discover what they perceive to be sacred to your relationship and set apart from other relationships. Your chart is one way for you to determine where your boundaries are and what types of comments or experiences nudge or cross your boundaries.

3. When have you nudged or crossed the boundaries of others?

Illustration 2.1

This is the chart that Pastor Shoshanna, a young married pastor with two children, designed for her ministry:

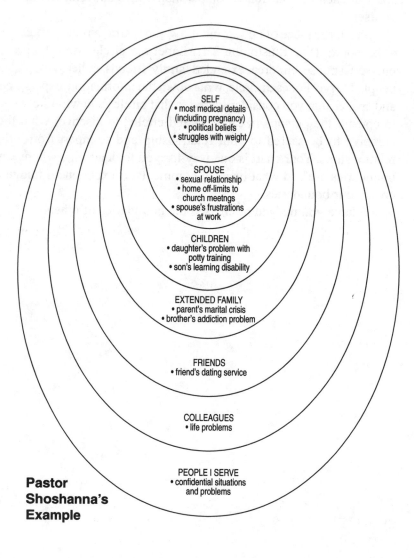

SELF
• most medical details
(including pregnancy)
• political beliefs
• struggles with weight

SPOUSE
• sexual relationship
• home off-limits to
church meetngs
• spouse's frustrations
at work

CHILDREN
• daughter's problem with
potty training
• son's learning disability

EXTENDED FAMILY
• parent's marital crisis
• brother's addiction problem

FRIENDS
• friend's dating service

COLLEAGUES
• life problems

PEOPLE I SERVE
• confidential situations
and problems

**Pastor
Shoshanna's
Example**

Connecting with a Partner

1. Use the following role-playing exercises to practice setting boundaries with people in your ministry setting.
   a. A congregant in the midst of a nasty separation from his wife shows up during your office hours at least twice a week. Once there, he spends an hour complaining about his wife, who is also a parishioner. He shows no interest in taking steps to overcome his bitterness or to resolve the conflicts with his wife. The time you are spending with this parishioner is keeping you from other important duties and you are feeling uncomfortable with his attempts to get you on his side against his wife. What do you say?
   b. At a church dinner, a congregant asks a personal question. Choose one or two of the following and tell how you would respond: Are you going to marry that person you've been dating? Are you pregnant? Are you ever going to have another child? Is that your real hair? So where did you get the money to buy that new cottage? Your child seems awfully rowdy, does he or she have some kind of learning disability?
   c. After vacation, a congregational leader approaches you and says, "While you were gone, we wanted to know what we did for that festival service last year. So, I looked through your desk and file drawers to get a copy of the service. I hope you don't mind."
   d. A parishioner who appears to be attracted to you insists on hugging you each time he or she sees you—after church, before meetings, and even alone in your office. What do you do?
2. What are some of your strategies for setting good boundaries?

Connecting with God

Hebrews 4:13 reads, "And before [God] no creature is hidden, but all are naked and laid bare to the eyes of the one to whom we must render an account." All of us have secret places that we keep apart from the eyes and ears of others. God is the only one privy to the whole of our lives. Thankfully, God looks upon us with kind and merciful eyes. This week, during your devotional time, confess to God those personal sins you are especially glad that others do not know about. Write them on chalkboard or sand. When you have finished, wash or sweep them away as a reminder that God forgives your sins and renews your life.

Challenge

Choose one boundary that is regularly violated by someone. Take steps to resolve the boundary violation this week.

Managing Unfinished Business

A friend of ours tells of his act of teenage rebellion. In his highly musical family, he would return home late at night and play the first seven notes of a scale on the family's piano. As the last note hung in the air, he would wait for one of his parents or siblings to come out of their bedroom and finish the scale. Someone always did. His family had trouble coping with unfinished business.

As a spiritual leader, you may feel that you are frequently beginning scales that do not get completed. Every day, you run out of time before you run out of tasks. There is always at least one more phone call, visit, or e-mail on your to-do list. As you juggle your responsibilities at work and in your personal life, you may never have a sense of completeness. Still, it is important to develop a strategy for managing all of the unfinished business. Then you can enjoy your time away from work without obsessing about all that remains to be done.

Connecting with Yourself

1. Unfinished business can drain your energy. The activities you leave undone may distract you from the tasks before you and even invade your dreams. In this exercise you will make a list of all of your unfinished business at work. When your list is complete, look at each task and ask yourself:
   - What is stopping me from getting this task done?
   - What would need to happen for me to finish this task?
2. Sometimes it is helpful to divide large tasks into several smaller tasks. Do this for any of the larger tasks on your list. (For example, Pastor

Lee needed to plan a Christmas Eve worship service. He divided the task into these steps: Review past Christmas Eve services, select theme for this year, choose texts, choose music, and write up bulletin for secretary.)

3. Next to each task on your list, indicate how much time you think it would take to finish this task.

4. Look at your calendar and assign a time to either delegate or complete each task. (And do it!)

Connecting with a Partner

1. Make a plan to support each other in completing your unfinished business. Here are some suggestions:
    a. Set aside a day to work independently on your unfinished business. Call each other at regular intervals to offer support.
    b. Set aside a time to work together at completing unfinished tasks.
    c. Get together to share ideas and information about delegating or completing tasks.
    d. Plan to meet at the end of a day of coping with unfinished business to enjoy a celebratory meal or activity.

2. Even when you complete most of the tasks on your to-do list, some tasks will still remain.
    *   How well do you handle the unfinished nature of your work?
    *   How often do you find yourself thinking about uncompleted tasks during your time off?
    *   How often do you dream about unfinished work or wake in the middle of the night remembering tasks you failed to complete?
        Brainstorm strategies for leaving unfinished work behind so that your time off can be more refreshing.

Connecting with God

This week develop one or two rituals to assist you in letting go of unfinished tasks as you move from your work into your personal life. You may want to use one of the following suggestions or create your own.
*   Leave a copy of your to-do list in a special box on your desk marked "In God's Hands."

- As you leave your workspace (which could be your office, your car, or a hospital room) say this prayer: *O God, into your hands I commend those tasks that I have not yet completed. Until I can return to them, I entrust these tasks and all whom they affect into your never-failing care.*

Challenge

One way to avoid a long list of unfinished business is to set up systems that will automatically provide you with an opportunity to finish tasks in a timely manner. For example, you might find it helpful to visit congregants who are homebound on the same days each month. You may set your computer date book to remind you when monthly or yearly tasks need to be completed (such as planning the fall schedule).

You might designate a certain time period each week for the purpose of "catching up" on tasks you have been avoiding. Another approach is to use a "worst first" system. Since most people tend to delay doing those tasks that they least enjoy, when you take time to catch up on your to-do list try completing the work you find least desirable before moving on to tasks you prefer.

This week look at your list of unfinished business and set up a system that will help prevent these tasks from languishing on your unfinished list again.

Responding to Praise and Blame

"Pastor, the stewardship drive was amazing this year—and we owe it all to you!"

"Rabbi, can you imagine—only three of us showed up for your new study on the historical background of the book of Habakkuk. What a failure!"

"You're the teacher—it all depends on you!"

As a leader who takes responsibility, you will gather bushels of both praise and blame in your ministry. Don't let it go to your head—or heart. And don't believe it all. Most of what people say about you has more to do with them than you. Still, you hear it, and you can't help but be influenced.

It is tempting to develop a ministry around the reactions of other people. Many spiritual leaders tend to do more of what the people they serve prefer them to do—whether it is healthy or not.

This week you will look at the effect that both praise and criticism have on your ministry. You will consider how to discern the truth in what you hear. You will remember that ultimately, your ministry is not defined by the judgments of others but by the grace of God.

Connecting with Yourself

1. In your journal make a list of some of the criticisms that you have received in your ministry; then, respond to the following questions.
   - How did you respond at the time?
   - Was there any truth in the statement? What was it?
   - What does the statement reveal about the speaker?
   - In what ways did the statement affect your approach to ministry?

2. Make a list of some of the compliments you have received in your ministry. How have you responded to them? What about these compliments has been helpful to you?
3. How much do you allow others' opinions of you and your actions to affect your thoughts, feelings, and actions?

    Are there types of comments or certain individuals whose comments have a greater effect on you?

Connecting with a Partner

1. Discuss how you have learned to cope with the following types of criticism. What responses and techniques have you found to be most effective, both in the moment and in your own subsequent processing of the event?
    - Hit and Run: On the way out of church someone criticizes you and leaves before you have a chance to respond.
    - Backhanded Compliment: Someone gives you a compliment that bears a criticism within it. "Your sermon was more engaging than it usually is."
    - Unsolicited Advice: This advice criticizes what you are doing or not doing. "I visited a church where the pastor made cookies for every visitor and delivered them herself. Maybe if you did that we would have more new members."
    - The Comparative Critique: This criticism compares you to the real or imagined actions of another person. "Our last pastor visited the congregants who were homebound every week."
    - The Anonymous Letter: This one is self-explanatory.
    - The Committee Ambush: A group of people make public complaints against you, usually without providing advance warning.
    - The Backstabber: You are criticized behind your back and you find out about it after the fact.
    - Everybody's Criticism: A criticism that begins with the phrase, "Everybody is saying . . ."
    - Consider any other types of criticism that you have experienced.
2. Criticisms and compliments can sway you from your goals and priorities. Does your response to praise and criticism tend to help or hinder your ministry? What can you do to keep yourself focused on your primary ministry tasks?

Connecting with God

Read through one of the four gospels and reflect on how Jesus responded to both praise and blame. How does knowing that Jesus received a great deal of criticism affect your approach to ministry? How can Jesus' actions serve as a guide for your ministry?

Challenge

While compliments should not totally shape one's ministry, spiritual leaders can gain much value from the praise of others. Many of us allow the kind words people utter to pass us by unnoticed. When we pay attention to these compliments, we can find encouragement for the work we do.

This week, pay special attention to the compliments you receive. Create a compliment box—a nicely decorated box filled with plain index cards. Use the index cards to write down the kind words of others. Make sure the box is large enough to hold the cards and letters you receive during your ministry. Keep the box in an accessible place to review on those days when you receive more criticism than praise.

Overhauling Your Work Space

Take a minute to look at the space or spaces in which you do most of your ministry work. Are you swimming in a sea of papers, having saved every dot and tittle since seminary? Or are you one of those who hasn't even kept last week's council minutes? People have different levels of tolerance for clutter and cleanliness. Still, your workspace must work for you. Your office needs to function so well that it silently supports you in ministry.

No matter what your workspace looks like, the exercises this week will help you to organize it in such a way that you can work more efficiently. If you have multiple workspaces, you will need to do these exercises for each space.

Connecting with Yourself

1. The first step toward creating the perfect workspace involves deciding how you want to use it. Look at your workspace and answer the following questions in your journal:
    - What are the tasks you need to accomplish in this space?
    - What tools do you need to complete these tasks?
    - What things inspire you while you work? (Examples might include music or mementos.)
    - What future tasks or activities would you like to make room for in this space?
2. In this exercise you will group your work-related possessions in terms of the tasks you wish to accomplish in your workspace. You may want to label cardboard boxes for this task (for example "preaching" or "administration"). Be sure to include extra boxes with labels such as

"toss," "charity," and "belongs elsewhere." You will review all of your work-related books, papers, mementos, and tools. Your goal is to toss everything that does not fit into your working plan. If you can answer yes to any of the following questions, then keep the item in question. If not, toss it.

- Is this item necessary and usable for the tasks you do or wish to do in your workspace?
- Is this item something that inspires you?
- Is this item something you ought to store "just in case" you might need it? (We don't recommend this. If you do feel a need for storage, put the item away. If you have not used it after six months, seriously consider tossing it then.)

3. Look at your workspace and assign "areas" for each of the tasks you wish to accomplish (or the tools for that task). For example, you may want to have areas for counseling, study, and administrative work. Include an area for the storage of current paperwork. You may want to organize your books and resources by topic. You may need to rearrange or toss furniture, and consider the purchase of new items.
4. Clean areas that are dirty.
5. Purchase containers or tools that will aid you in organizing your office. You may also want to find items that either inspire or comfort you. Consider art for your walls, a place for music, perhaps candles or incense, a comfortable chair—anything that might nurture and inspire you in your work and ministry. Once you have secured these items, put your workspace back together and then get rid of the excess without a second look.

Connecting with a Partner

1. If tossing your beloved possessions is painful to you, you may want to enlist your partner's help with this task.
2. If you prefer to work alone, utilize your partner for moral support. Plan a day to work on this at the same time and then call each other at agreed-upon intervals for encouragement.
3. When you have finished your work, do something to celebrate together.

Connecting with God

With your partner and other trusted friends and family, arrange to have a "workspace blessing" ceremony. You may choose to bring candles, incense, and music to enhance your ceremony. The section titled "Blessings" in the appendix includes resources that can help you.

Challenge

Your first challenge was getting your office in shape. The bigger challenge will be keeping it clean and orderly. Decide on a set time each week that you will use to maintain the order of your workspace. This will be the time when you clean up the papers, books, and mail that clutter your desk. You may also use this time to clean and dust surfaces. In short, you will do what you can to keep your workspace working for you.

Celebrating Successes

If you are like many spiritual leaders, your ministry may feel like an endless to-do list. You may work through your days always thinking, "So what's next on the agenda?" You preach a great sermon on Sunday and then wake up on Monday to start a new one. You get through the Advent-Christmas season of activities only to realize that Lent looms around the corner. You complete a successful Bible study and someone asks, "When does the next study begin?"

Because of the nature of their work, many spiritual leaders rarely take time to savor their accomplishments. Making time in your schedule to express gratitude for the blessings you have experienced and to celebrate your accomplishments can bring joy and a renewed sense of purpose to your ministry.

Connecting with Yourself

1. Make a list of the activities and experiences that bring you joy and are potential vehicles for celebration. Your list can include activities you might do alone or with others and range from short to long, inexpensive to costly. Use your journal and try to come up with as many as possible. Examples include a bubble bath, a massage, a trip to your favorite bookstore, a night at the movies, a nap, a hot-fudge sundae, a dinner gathering with friends, a pool party, a ski trip, or a walk in the park.
2. Make a list of occasions that you might choose to celebrate in the next year (alone, or with colleagues, parishioners, family, or friends). Include both big accomplishments (such as completing your stewardship drive)

and small ones (such as preaching a good sermon or finishing a month of shut-in visits). Here are some other suggestions:

- Celebrate the date of your ordination anniversary (or the anniversary of your beginning to work in your current ministry setting or the anniversary of your baptismal date).
- Count up the number of baptisms, weddings, or sermons that have been a part of your current call or lifetime in ministry. Decide on a number that you want to celebrate and when you get there—do so.
- Celebrate the beginning and end of church seasons.
- Celebrate the beginning and end of Bible studies or other classes.

3. Schedule at least one celebration for each of the next six months in your calendar. Write down what you will celebrate and how you will celebrate it. Contact those people you want to include in your celebrations. If any events need extra planning, use a calendar to make notes to yourself about when to follow through on those plans.

Connecting with a Partner

1. Talk about the role of celebration in your life and ministry. (Is it something that comes easily? Why or why not? Do you celebrate often? Why or why not?)
2. How does taking time to reflect on or savor your accomplishments affect your attitude toward your life and ministry?
3. Share three accomplishments from your ministry.

Connecting with God

Let your devotional time take on a celebratory tone this week. Thank God for blessing your life and ministry. Share with God those life and ministry accomplishments for which you are most grateful. Be creative in the ways you express your gratitude. You may use one of these ideas or come up with one of your own:

- Write a psalm of praise.
- Dance your praise to a favorite hymn or song, using scarves or other tools of expression.

- Paint a visual expression of your praise.
- Build something from clay, wood, or even sand that reflects your gratitude.
- Bake bread and share it with others in gratitude to God.
- Light candles or incense during your prayers.

Challenge

Celebrate some accomplishment in your work this week. You can celebrate alone or with friends, family, or parishioners—just celebrate. Enjoy yourself, and thank God for blessing your ministry

Week Nineteen

Retreat Week

This retreat week provides another opportunity and a new setting from which to consider your working life. Refer to the introduction for a description of the purpose and structure of a retreat week. As you create a retreat that is nurturing for you, you may want to use some of the following movies, books, and activities.

MOVIES AND VIDEO

The Apostle
A flamboyant Pentecostal minister with a bad temper starts a new church in poverty-stricken Louisiana.

The Bishop's Wife
An overwhelmed bishop and his wife receive help from an angel.

The Crowd
This classic silent movie provides insights into the sometimes meaningless world of work.

The Farmer's Wife (A David Sutherland Film)
This PBS special follows the life of a young farmer's wife as she struggles to manage the farm, raise a family, and attend school.

Heavens Above
An idealistic vicar seeks to accomplish his ministry despite the resistance of his parishioners.

Livelyhood
This PBS series about how people work today is available at many public libraries and for purchase at www.pbs.org/livelyhood/videotapes.html.

Mass Appeal
A priest and a seminarian clash over ideology.

What about Bob?
A neurotic psychiatric patient tests the boundaries of his newest doctor, who is on vacation.

BOOKS

Fiction

Crampton Hodnet by Barbara Pym
A priest in a British village learns that his private life is not so private.

Father Melancholy's Daughter and *Evensong* by Gail Godwin
These two novels follow Margaret Gower. In the first, she and her father, an Episcopal priest, struggle with Margaret's mother's desertion. In the second, Pastor Margaret Gower ministers in her own small congregation.

The Good News from North Haven by Michael Lindvall
This series of stories features a small-town Minnesota pastor as he confronts the challenges of parish ministry.

The Handyman by Carolyn See
A painter, before he becomes famous, takes on various "handyman" jobs to fund his painting and appears to have a vocation for caring for others.

The Little Red Hen by Paul Galdone
Revisit this classic children's tale about not wanting to take responsibility for work.

"A List" in *Frog and Toad Together* by Arnold Lobel
In this children's story, the characters learn about how list making affects their day.

Lyddie by Katherine Paterson
In this novel for middle-grade readers, Lyddie Warthen, a Vermont farm girl, works in a factory in Lowell, Massachusetts.

Rookery Blues and *The Dean's List* by Jon Hassler
In these two novels, Hassler follows a small group of professors through both their professional and their personal lives at a small state college in Minnesota.

The Soloist by Mark Salzman
A gifted musician's vocation is tested when he loses the ability to perform.

The Three Little Pigs by Paul Galdone
A trio of swine learn about how the quality of one's work can affect one's life in this well-known story for children.

Nonfiction

The Active Life: A Spirituality of Work, Creativity, and Caring by Parker J. Palmer
This book explores the relationship between work and reflection while gaining insights from classic stories and poems.

Bird by Bird: Reflections on Writing and Life by Anne Lamott
Lamott's often-humorous reflections about the writing life apply well to the tasks inherent in both life and ministry.

The Living Reminder: Service and Prayer in Memory of Jesus Christ by Henri J. M. Nouwen
Nouwen writes about how Jesus' life and ministry can form the framework for our own ministry.

The Sabbath by Abraham Joshua Heschel
This classic study of the Jewish concept of sabbath, first published in 1951, continues to remind readers of the sacredness of time.

The Seven Habits of Highly Effective People by Stephen Covey
Covey's best-selling book on managing time and setting priorities provides helpful advice to people juggling multiple tasks.

The Sewing Room: Uncommon Reflection on Life, Love, and Work by Rev. Barbara Cawthorn Crafton
An Episcopal priest reflects on her ministry with people from all walks of life in New York City.

The Three Boxes of Life by Richard N. Bolles
Bolles believes that life's three boxes—learning, working, and playing—need to be lived simultaneously instead of sequentially.

Working the Angles: The Shape of Pastoral Integrity by Eugene H. Peterson
Peterson encourages spiritual leaders to make prayer, scripture, and spiritual direction priorities in their ministry.

ACTIVITIES

- If you do not already do so, take a traditional Sabbath—from sundown to sundown. (You may want to consult a book or a colleague about how to do this.)
- Take a daylong (or as much time as you can spare) sabbatical from all forms of media and electronic communication (no books, no phones). You might choose to make this a silent retreat.
- Read a biography or watch a documentary about a spiritual leader (either historical or contemporary) whom you admire.
- Explore an area of ministry that you are interested in but rarely have time to think about.
- Attend a public performance (such as a play or orchestra) or sporting event. What can you as a spiritual leader learn from other "public performers"?
- Ask some retired people to share any insights they have gained about work since retirement.
- Observe animals or insects working together—in your backyard, at the local zoo, or on video. What lessons can you learn from their habits?
- Read the book of Ecclesiastes. Reflect on the insights it brings to your ministry.
- Take a retreat with your colleagues from work and do something fun together. (Try an activity like playing miniature golf or board games.)

Do not allow any work or conversation about work or the people you serve.

- Visit the Web site www.familiesandworkinst.org for current research on balancing work and family.
- Do an Internet search on work styles or work style inventory. Many career services provide free tools to help you discover more about your working style.

Section Three

Nurturing Your Relationships

Revisiting Your Family of Origin

When Pastor Joe started in his first parish as a single man, he often received gifts of food from Mrs. Davis. "You remind me of my son," she said. Mrs. Davis's son lived far away and so she spent her motherly efforts doting on Pastor Joe. He didn't mind. Mrs. Davis's kind gestures reminded him of his own mother who had died a few years before.

The way you function in all of your relationships (including those in your ministry setting) is influenced by the patterns of relating you developed in your family of origin. Many of us are unaware of the power these foundational relationships carry in our adult lives. Gaining knowledge about how our early relationships have shaped and continue to influence our lives can aid us in our current relationships.

As a child, you may have created a "family tree" that included the names of several generations of your family. This week's focus centers around a similar task—creating a more detailed version of your family tree called a genogram.

Connecting with Yourself

1. In this exercise, you will create a multigenerational genogram—beginning with your generation and working backward. Your genogram will depict a great deal of information about you and your family. It might be helpful to gather the information first and then create your genogram chart on a piece of tag board or newsprint using the symbols explained below.

    If possible, try to gather information about five generations of your family. Include as much of the following information as possible: names, current ages, birth dates, death dates, marriages, divorces, adopted or foster children, pregnancies, miscarriages, stillbirths, abortions, medical conditions (examples include alcoholism and cancer), emotional conditions (examples include anxiety and depression), places of residence, occupations, and educational levels.

The following symbols tell you how to depict the information on your genogram. Note that on a genogram, birth order is depicted from left to right, starting with the oldest child. Identify yourself with either a double circle or a double square.

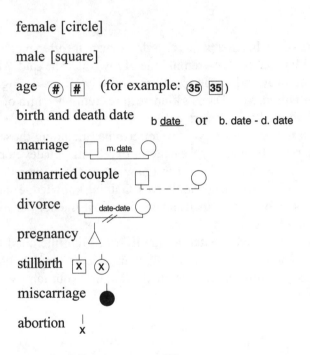

female [circle]

male [square]

age (for example:)

birth and death date b date or b. date - d. date

marriage

unmarried couple

divorce

pregnancy

stillbirth

miscarriage

abortion

An example follows on page 77.

Illustration 3.1

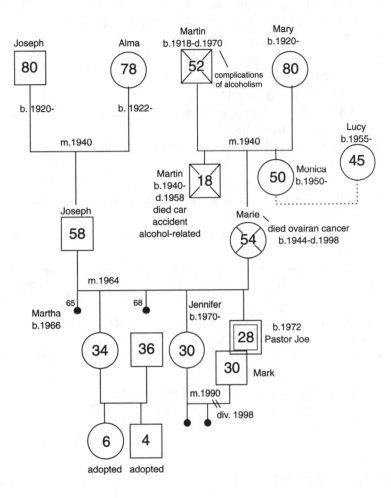

2. Once you have completed the genogram, reflect on the following questions in your journal:
    -   What traits or abilities did you receive from your family of origin?
    -   To whom did you feel the closest while growing up?
    -   With whom did you experience emotional distance?
    -   Whom did you most admire?
    -   Who had the most influence over you?
    -   In whom were you able to confide?
    -   What role did church, religion, or spirituality play in the lives of your family members?
    -   From whom did you find the greatest support in your decision to become a spiritual leader?
    -   From whom did you experience the most opposition?
    -   With whom did you have conflict? What issues or situations were involved in the conflict?
    -   As you scan your genogram, what patterns do you observe in your family?

3. How would you characterize the roles you played in your family of origin? (For example, if you were the firstborn of several children and you frequently took on responsibilities for your siblings, you might characterize yourself as a caretaker. Other types of roles might include peacemaker, overachiever, clown, or troublemaker.)
    -   How have these roles affected your self-image and the choices you have made?
    -   What roles do you play in your congregation?
    -   How do these roles compare to the roles you played in your family of origin?

Connecting with a Partner

1. Using your genogram, take 20 to 30 minutes to tell your family's story. When each of you has finished, take 10 to 15 minutes to respond to your partner's genogram. You can use the response time to ask questions or share insights.
2. In what ways have your relationships in your family of origin affected your relationships with your friends, with your family of choice, and with people in your ministry setting?

Connecting with God

Choose a trait or ability that you have in common with one of your family members. Perhaps you have Uncle Arthur's sense of humor or Aunt Elizabeth's ear for music. During your devotional time, thank God for this gift that was passed down to you through the generations.

Find a way to celebrate this gift. Share it with others in a purposeful way. Indulge in it in a new way. For example, if you are a gifted musician, you might use your gift to teach others to love music. If you are a gifted swimmer, but haven't had time to be near water, make time to swim in the next week.

Challenge

Contact a family member with whom you have not spoken for a while. Tell this person about the work you are doing to learn about your family of origin. Set a time this week to begin a conversation (via phone, e-mail, or in person) about your experiences in your family of origin.

Approaching Conflict Effectively

Wherever two or three are gathered . . . there's bound to be a disagreement eventually. Conflict happens. It is an inevitable consequence of all relationships, both in personal life and ministry. The key to maintaining healthy relationships lies not in avoiding conflict, but in handling conflict in a healthy manner. This week you will work at strengthening your personal and professional relationships by considering the most effective ways to approach conflict in your life and ministry.

Connecting with Yourself

1. Much of what you know about handling conflict, you learned in your family of origin. When you moved into new relationships beyond your family of origin, you were exposed to other styles of coping with conflict. Reflect on the following questions in your journal:
   - How was conflict handled in your family of origin?
   - What roles did you play as a child in conflicts in your family of origin?
   - What roles do you currently play in conflicts with your family of origin?
2. In your journal, write about two recent experiences with conflict, one that is personal (with a friend, family member, or stranger) and one that is ministry related. Record what happened both during the conflict and its resolution. When you have finished, respond to these questions:
   - What were you feeling internally during the course of the conflict and its resolution?

- What physical symptoms did you experience during the conflict and its resolution?
- How satisfied did you feel with the resolution?
- As you look back on how you handled the conflict, what did you do well?
- If you could relive the situation, what would you say or do differently?
- How does your approach to conflict in these situations compare with how you learned to deal with conflict in your family of origin?

3. Spiritual leaders often encounter conflicts involving a disagreement between two other parties. The spiritual leader gets drawn into the argument, creating a triangle. A triangle is a connection that is formed anytime a person talks to you about another person with whom they have a relationship. This conversation may not be malevolent, but it does always carry with it the possibility of creating conflict. For example, a concerned daughter might approach you about her mother's health care rather than speaking directly to her mother.

    Long-term triangles are created when this method of relating becomes a pattern over time. This can be difficult for you as the third person because you end up bearing the responsibility of having too much information and input into a relationship that you are not a part of. In the above example, it might mean that over time this daughter agonizes with you over every medical decision she makes for her mother. Her anxiety becomes a part of your daily life. For some people, being in this situation can be greatly energizing—they feel helpful, important, and connected. Even so, when two people in a relationship connect primarily about a third party, their relationship is less than healthy.

    Using your journal, make a list of the triangles that you are currently a part of. These triangles might be in your family of origin, with your friends, or at work.

- In what ways does being a part of these triangles affect your life?
- In what ways does being a part of these triangles affect your relationships with the people in the triangles?
- How would not participating in the triangle affect your relationships with each person in the triangle?

Connecting with a Partner

1. What types of triangles do you find most difficult to get out of? What techniques have you adopted for staying out of triangles?
2. Look at each of the following unhelpful ways of coping with conflict and discuss the following questions for each approach. Discuss any other unhelpful approaches you have witnessed or used.
    *   In what types of conflict situations are you most tempted to use this approach?
    *   When other people use this approach with you, what would be the best way to respond?
    *   What are the long-term consequences of repeatedly using this approach?
        a. Denial: "I am going to pretend this conflict doesn't exist."
        b. No compromises: "Come hell or high water, I won't give in."
        c. Passive Peacekeeping: "I don't want to rock the boat; just do whatever you want."
        d. Avoidance: "You all figure it out; just don't involve me."
        e. Passive-Aggressive: Now: "I don't care what happens." Later: "I had a feeling this wouldn't work."
        f. Overresponse: "Oh, my, Mrs. Johnson's angry again. Let's do whatever it takes to placate her."
        g. My way or the highway: "If you don't do what I want, I'm transferring my membership to another church."
3. Describe a conflict situation from your own life that you wish you had handled differently. With your partner, either role-play the situation or talk through how you would handle it now. Attempt to create a situation in which all parties feel heard and a solution that allows each party to be a winner.
4. Conflicts are inevitable, yet you can choose which battles to engage in. What personal values or standards are you willing to adhere to even if conflict results?

Connecting with God

Make an effort this week to pray each day for those with whom you are experiencing conflict. Ask God for the wisdom and compassion you need to approach conflict in a way that nurtures your relationships. If you are not currently experiencing conflict with anyone, pray for those with whom you have experienced conflict in the past.

Challenge

This week, whenever you become aware of someone talking to you about someone else, encourage that person to share their comments with the appropriate party. For example, you might say to your father, "I think Mom needs to know how you feel." You might mention to a friend who regularly complains about a coworker, "I think Jen would be helped by hearing what you think about her job performance."

Improving Communication Skills

Somebody once asked a great preacher what enabled her to speak so effectively to her parishioners. She replied, "I'm a good listener."

As a spiritual leader, you are no doubt aware that the skills of speaking and listening are intimately connected. Good communication forms the cornerstone of dynamic ministries and healthy relationships. Still, none of us are perfect practitioners of the art of communication. No relationship is immune from the possibility of misunderstanding. Because of the ever-changing nature of human interactions, communication skills require constant practice and perfecting. This week you will look at the communication patterns you developed in your family of origin and work on improving both your speaking and your listening skills.

Connecting with Yourself

1. Recall sitting at the family dinner table or some other setting where family conversations took place when you were a child. In your journal reflect on the following questions:
    *   Who initiated conversations?
    *   What topics were spoken about?
    *   What topics were off-limits?
    *   Who spoke most and least frequently?
    *   How much personal disclosure took place?
    *   What was your role in the conversations?
    *   Which members of your family listened to you?
    *   What cues did you have that members of your family listened to you or didn't listen to you?

2. Think about the conversations you have on a daily basis, both personally and professionally. Reflect on the following questions:
    *   With whom do you communicate easily? What factors do you attribute that to?
    *   With whom do you have difficulty communicating? What factors do you attribute that to?
    *   How does your current communication style reflect the patterns you observed or exhibited in your family of origin?
    *   Are there patterns you would like to change?
    *   What steps could you take to change those patterns?
3. Choose a day this week to pay particular attention to your listening skills. At the end of the day, review the following list and check the listening habits you exhibited during the day. Note when and with whom you used each habit. When you have finished reviewing the list, consider which of these habits you might let go of or adapt to improve your listening skills.

    When another person is speaking, I am . . .

    _____ thinking about what to say next.
    _____ listening for how what the speaker is saying relates to me.
    _____ looking for the next best person to speak with.
    _____ reviewing a list of tasks in my head.
    _____ thinking about the conversation I just had with someone else.
    _____ paying attention to nonverbal cues from the speaker.
    _____ interrupting.
    _____ appreciating the speaker's story.
    _____ making judgments about what the speaker is saying.
    _____ watching the clock.
    _____ asking questions to gain a deeper understanding of the speaker.
    _____ ignoring ideas and information I don't want to hear.
    _____ attempting to categorize the speaker into a framework I understand.
    _____ using nonverbal language to communicate my empathy with the speaker.
    _____ making eye contact with the speaker.
    _____ thinking about when would be a good time to exit the conversation.
    _____ trying to physically escape from the conversation.

_____ trying to change the topic of conversation.

_____ thinking of a way to solve the speaker's problems.

_____ waiting for an opportunity to criticize or reprimand the person.

_____ making physical contact with the person.

_____ making mental or actual notes of what the person has said for future reference.

_____ other

Connecting with a Partner

1. What are the cues that indicate someone is listening to you?
2. Think about a difficult conversation that you would like to have with another person in your life. (It does not have to be a conversation that you actually plan to have.) Role-play that conversation with your partner. When you have finished, give each other feedback on both speaking and listening skills.

Connecting with God

Spend at least 10 minutes each day this week listening for God. You may want to begin the time by reading this verse, "Speak, for your servant is listening" (1 Sam. 3:10b). Other passages that may serve as a good beginning to your listening time are: 1 Kings 19:11-13; Ps. 29:3-11; John 10:3-4; and Rev. 21:3-4.

Challenge

Set up a weekly meeting with both your family and your coworkers. Use the time to plan your schedules, clarify expectations, discuss difficult situations, and celebrate successes. Provide adequate time for each person to speak about each issue. Choose a setting that is comfortable for all. Food and beverages may help to make the experience more enjoyable. If conversation is difficult, the resources *Growing Together: Spiritual Exercises for Church Committees* and *Difficult Conversations: Taking Risks, Acting with Integrity* (listed under "Committees" and "Conflict" in the appendix) might help guide the process.

Recognizing and Expressing Feelings

On a chilly autumn night, Father Phil built a beautiful fire in the vicarage fireplace. He didn't know that the birds had built an equally beautiful nest on top of the flue, preventing it from opening. Instead of rising out of the top of the chimney, the smoke from the fire came streaming into the house.

Feelings in the body may be compared to smoke in a chimney. They have to come out somewhere. When feelings are not expressed in healthy and appropriate ways, they often reveal themselves in more destructive manners such as impulsive actions, health problems, or boundary crossing.

Feelings both reflect and affect one's life. They provide clues to the condition of one's life and ministry. They can also affect how one experiences the events of daily life. The purpose of this week's activities is not to seek to alter your moods or feelings, but to help you learn to discern what you are feeling and express it appropriately. If the work this week creates a strong emotional reaction for you, consider consulting a therapist.

Connecting with Yourself

The following list of feelings will be used in this week's exercises. Add any feelings that you think are missing.

abandoned	ecstatic	loving
affectionate	embarrassed	overwhelmed
afraid	empathic	passionate
alienated	encouraged	peaceful
ambitious	energetic	playful

ambivalent	excited	pleased
amused	exhausted	protective
angry	foolish	proud
annoyed	frustrated	refreshed
anxious	grateful	relieved
apathetic	grieved	resentful
ashamed	grumpy	resigned
bereft	guilty	sad
bitter	happy	satisfied
bored	hassled	secure
compassionate	hateful	seductive
confident	hesitant	self-conscious
confused	honored	sensual
content	hopeful	sexually aroused
creative	hopeless	shy
critical	humble	silly
delighted	humiliated	smart
depressed	hurt	strong
despondent	ignored	sullen
disappointed	impatient	surprised
discontented	inadequate	tired
disgusted	irritated	trusting
distraught	jealous	vulnerable
distressed	joyful	worried
doubtful	lonely	

1. Record your answers to the following questions in your journal. In this exercise, it is important that you write down your first reaction and not analyze your answers.

    Look at the list of feelings.
    • Which feelings do you have trouble accepting in yourself?
    • Which feelings do you have difficulty expressing?
    Make a list of the five feelings that you most commonly experience.
    • Which feelings do you have difficulty accepting or responding to in others?
    • Which feelings are you comfortable responding to in others?
2. If you could use two or three feeling words to describe your family of origin, which would they be?

- Which feelings did you feel comfortable expressing in your family of origin?
- Which feelings, if any, did you have difficulty expressing in your family of origin? Why?
- Which feelings brought your family closer together?
- Which feelings resulted in your family becoming more distant?

3. Feelings affect our interaction with self, God, and others. Many times we don't even realize how they are impacting us. This exercise is designed to help you consider the range of feelings you experience in a day. Make a copy of the feeling checklist above. Carry it with you throughout the day.
   - At the end of each activity or at each hour, make a note of the feelings you experienced during the past event or the past hour.
   - Record what you were doing at the time you experienced that feeling.
   - What physical symptoms accompanied the feeling (examples include sweaty palms, racing heart, and flushed face)?
   - At the end of the day, look over your record. Do you notice any patterns? Do certain types of activities or interactions tend to trigger specific kinds of feelings? What are your feelings telling you about these activities or interactions?

4. The following is a journaling tool to help you accept and express your feelings.

   After an event or interaction that draws strong feelings from you, record your answers to the following questions in your journal:
   - What was the situation?
   - What were the feelings you experienced?
   - What physical symptoms accompanied the feelings?
   - What were you thinking at the time?
   - What did you say or do?
   - What, if anything, do you wish you would have said or done differently?

   If, at this point, the situation still feels unresolved, consider what can you do now to resolve it.

Connecting with a Partner

1. In general, what has your faith tradition taught you about feelings?
    *   Which feelings are acceptable in your faith tradition?
    *   Which feelings are either unacceptable or unexpressed in your faith tradition?
2. Describe your ministry setting in terms of feelings.
    *   What five feeling words describe the type of setting in which you serve?
    *   How do these feelings get expressed in your ministry setting?
    *   What skills have you had to learn or do you need to learn to respond to the feelings that are expressed in your ministry setting?

Connecting with God

Use the feeling words in the list above in your spoken prayers to God.

Challenge

A study at the State University of New York at Stony Brook School of Medicine by Dr. Joshua M. Smyth suggests that writing about difficult life experiences can prove healing to the writer. In the study, patients were instructed to write about stressful life events for 20 minutes a day, three days a week. The study lasted for four months. As a result, 47 percent of the asthma patients showed improved lung function (*Asthma Free in Twenty-one Days* by Kathryn Shafer and Fran Greenfield, p. 139).

Using your journal, write about a stressful event in your life on three consecutive days for 20 minutes each day. (Some people choose to write about a death, the loss of a relationship, the diagnosis of an illness, or a significant life change.) Write without concern for how your work reads or what it says. Do not show your work to others or discuss the process with others. (If you are tired of journaling, use a tape recorder to record your thoughts surrounding the difficult event.)

If you find this activity helpful, consider continuing it on an ongoing basis.

Coping with Toxic Relationships

The word *toxic* may bring to mind poisonous substances such as asbestos and arsenic. We often hear the word used in connection to products, environments, and foods that can harm our health. In recent years, psychotherapists have connected this word to harmful relationships and to people who function in ways that are damaging to themselves and others.

Most people can identify individuals who behave in toxic ways. Conversations with them leave you feeling battered. They may repeatedly use abusive words, shower you with unsolicited advice, or simply encourage you to join their pity party. Their presence in your day can drain your energy and dampen your enthusiasm.

Because spiritual leaders relate to such a large number of people, their chances of being in contact with people who behave in a toxic manner are higher than the average individual. Unlike a store clerk or a physician, the spiritual leader's relationship with these individuals is typically more than a passing encounter. When your colleagues and the people you serve behave in toxic ways, both duty and your spiritual framework may dictate continuing your relationships with them. This week's exercises will give you an opportunity to define the toxic relationships in both your personal life and ministry and make decisions about how to cope with them.

Connecting with Yourself

1. In this exercise, you will review a checklist of ways in which people may behave in a toxic manner. This is not a complete list. You may add your own "toxic characteristics." As you look at the list, use your journal to note relationships in both your personal life and ministry that

are toxic. Make note of the person's name, his or her relationship to you, and the ways in which you have experienced the relationship to be toxic. When you have completed the list, place an asterisk next to the relationships that are primary in your life.

As you make this list, keep the following points in mind. First, while all people behave immaturely from time to time, some individuals have a pattern of relating in a toxic manner. Second, noting that these people are toxic in your life does not imply that they are in any way inferior or evil. This is simply an acknowledgment that they have developed patterns of relating with you that are unhealthy. Sometimes these patterns will be particular to your relationship, other times they are patterns that the individual carries to all of her or his relationships. Finally, as you work on a solution, remember that while people who behave in a toxic manner do have the ability to change their behavior, you do not hold either the responsibility or the power to change it for them.

An individual who is toxic to you is someone who repeatedly . . .

- criticizes you
- makes jokes at your expense
- makes sarcastic remarks
- belittles things, activities, or people that you value
- does not listen to you
- gives unsolicited advice
- verbally abuses you
- takes advantage of you
- brings up your past mistakes
- fails to respect your boundaries
- encourages you to engage in self-destructive behaviors
- sabotages your plans or efforts to take care of yourself or your needs
- breaks promises
- expects you to meet his or her unspoken needs
- threatens you
- attempts to control you
- uses praise to manipulate you
- gossips to or about you
- refuses to take responsibility for her or his own life
- complains
- blames others for his or her problems

- physically or sexually abuses you
- makes a catastrophe of daily events
- lies to you

2. Using your family genogram and your journal, reflect on how you learned to deal with toxic behavior in your childhood.
   - Identify the toxic relationships and behaviors that you witnessed or experienced as a child.
   - Make a list of the ways in which you saw your family members cope with these behaviors. (For example, accepted, enabled, invited, ignored, or normalized.)
   - Make a list of the ways in which you dealt with these toxic behaviors as a child and adolescent.

3. Once you have identified the toxic relationships in your life, you can consider how you want to handle them. Some options are listed below. Review the options and identify which ones you would use for particular relationships. You will have an opportunity to practice some of these techniques with a partner and use them in the single-step challenge.
   - As difficult as it may be, remember that this person is a child of God. Pray for this person.
   - Don't personalize this person's behavior. (Her or his actions and comments are not about you, even when they are directed at you in the form of criticism. These behaviors reflect the personal distress of the person engaging in them.)
   - Limit contact.
   - Have contact in groups only.
   - Attempt not to react to the person's behavior. (For example, do not encourage the person to continue to gossip by asking questions. Your lack of a reaction may temper his or her need to be toxic with you.)
   - Balance your time with the person by spending time with those who energize you.
   - Communicate to the person what you will not tolerate in your relationship. (For example, you might tell someone who constantly complains that you prefer not to hear the complaints unless she or he wants your help in planning to take action about them. This action may need to be taken more than once as the person learns how to be with you without behaving in a toxic manner.)

- Ask the person to join you in either therapy or mediation to work out your difficulties. This is especially helpful in primary relationships.
- Take a sabbatical from the relationship. Avoid contact with the person for awhile with the possibility of reestablishing contact in the future. You may or may not want to discuss this with the person.
- End the relationship, if it is possible. As you do this, consider the following questions:
  — Is this best done in person, on the phone, or through a letter?
  — How can you do this without condemning or labeling the other person?
  — How much do you need or want to share about how you feel?

4. In what ways might you be toxic in your relationships with others? What can you do to eliminate or minimize these behaviors?

Connecting with a Partner

1. Discuss or role-play how you might deal with the following toxic situations:
    a. Your ministry colleague repeatedly makes sarcastic remarks and jokes about your work in front of others.
    b. You return from vacation when you find out that once again Dave, a very needy parishioner, has left multiple messages for you. When you call Dave, he says, "Where have you been? You're never around when I need you."
    c. A friend repeatedly complains about her life, blaming everyone for her circumstances and failing to take responsibility for any part of her life. You have tried, on numerous occasions, to offer suggestions and support. To each offer, she responds, "Yes, but that would not work because . . ."

2. Choose one of the toxic relationships from your own life that you would like to work on. Briefly outline the situation for your partner and together consider strategies for handling the situation. You might want to role-play any discussion you plan to have with the toxic individual. Focus your time on working out a solution instead of talking about the person and the problem.

Connecting with God

Begin each day praying that God will give you the ability to recognize your own toxic behaviors and help you to eliminate them from your life. End each day praying for those people whose behaviors have been toxic to you.

Challenge

Take the steps necessary to deal with one of the toxic relationships you have identified. If this is a new experience for you, it will be easier to begin with the relationships that are least important to you. As you work through coping with other toxic relationships, especially those that are primary in your life, it might be helpful to consult with a therapist.

Week Twenty-Five

Understanding Anger

After we spoke on the topic of anger, a pastor approached us and said, "I'm not sure why you're talking about this. I never get angry. Sometimes I feel disappointed—but never angry."

During a Bible study, after disclosing our own struggles with anger, a parishioner said, "Come on, pastors, we know you'd never get really angry. I cannot imagine it!"

Despite Jesus' open expressions of anger, some spiritual leaders deny or ignore this part of their emotional life. They may be enabled in this task by the strong beliefs of their parishioners, colleagues, and friends that spiritual leaders should not feel or express anger.

Like conflict, anger is an inevitable consequence of human interaction. Sometimes anger is expressed in healthy ways. For others, it is displaced onto cars and family members. Still others use self-righteousness or martyrdom as an outlet for their anger. This week you will look at your own relationship to anger. You will consider what triggers it, how you express it, and how you can use anger in ways that are helpful and healthy for both you and your relationships.

Connecting with Yourself

1. The following is a checklist of some of the ways that anger can manifest itself. Check all of the ways that you express anger, adding any that are not on the list.

    _____ screaming

    _____ aggressive behavior (such as throwing things or driving recklessly)

_____ violent behavior (hitting, kicking, punching)
_____ passive aggression
_____ self-destructive thoughts
_____ self-destructive behavior (overeating, alcoholism, cutting)
_____ self-righteousness
_____ silence
_____ displacement onto objects or others
_____ clenched fists
_____ clenched jaw
_____ sighing
_____ crying
_____ shaking
_____ swearing
_____ arguing
_____ disengagement
_____ pouting

2. Using your journal, reflect on the following questions:
    - What were the typical ways people expressed anger in your family of origin?
    - What did your family members tend to get angry about?
    - In what ways were you allowed to express anger in your family of origin?
    - What did you tend to get angry about?

3. Recall five incidents from the past year when you felt angry. Write briefly about each in your journal. As you do so, answer the following questions for each situation:
    - What or who triggered your anger?
    - What physical symptoms of anger did you experience? (Examples might include a clenched jaw, stomach or back tension, headache, or rapid heartbeat.)
    - What else were you feeling besides anger? (For example, you might have felt hurt, betrayed, slighted, ridiculed, disappointed, afraid, or exhausted.)
    - What issue was behind your anger? (An example of an issue might be that someone inappropriately crossed your boundaries.)

    Review all five situations and the answers to the questions. What patterns do you see?

4.   The following list of behaviors can be helpful tools for coping with and expressing anger in healthy and helpful ways. Read through the Anger Toolbox list and reflect on the following questions:
     • Which of these are part of your "anger toolbox"?
     • What other strategies do you use to cope with anger?
     • In what ways could you see yourself utilizing these tools the next time someone or something triggers your anger?

Anger Toolbox
     deep breathing
     artistic expression of feelings: writing, drawing, painting, crafting
     physical activity: running, cleaning, lifting weights
     prayer
     relaxation exercises
     listening to soothing music
     reading scripture
     extreme self-care: shower, massage, rest
     talking through feelings with a friend
     discovering what triggered the anger
     understanding feelings and issues beneath the anger
     expressing feelings to the source of your anger

Connecting with a Partner

1.   What messages about expressing anger have you received from the following sources: your seminary, your superiors, your colleagues, people in your current ministry setting? How does the method in which people express anger in your current ministry setting compare to how anger was expressed in your family of origin?
2.   Recall a situation in which you felt that you expressed your anger in an unhelpful or unhealthy manner. Brainstorm better strategies of handling the situation.
3.   How do you typically respond to others when they are angry? Discuss strategies for coping with the anger of others.

Connecting with God

The psalmists provided great examples of how we can express all of our feelings to God, including anger. Express your anger, current or unresolved, to God. You may want to use a psalm, write one of your own, draw a picture that expresses your feelings, or throw stones into a lake (rather than the more expensive option of church windows) while speaking your piece.

Challenge

Unresolved anger can cause a multitude of relational and health problems. Resolving those situations can bring you a great sense of freedom. Choose one situation in your life in which you hold unresolved feelings of anger. Either resolve it or take steps to resolve it by using tools from the Anger Toolbox or some other strategy. Note that it is not always necessary that you resolve the situation with the other person—you can do it by yourself. This exercise is intended to help you let go of angry feelings that might be harmful to your own health or getting in the way of your own growth.

Pastor Brad wrote a long letter to members of a former parish that had acted abusively toward him. In it, he listed all of his grievances toward them. He expressed regret for his own reactionary behavior. He asked God to help him forgive those who wronged him. When he finished, he destroyed the letter and commended the situation to God.

Sister Judy sat down with a member of her community and expressed feelings of anger that had been bubbling for almost a year. The two sisters were able to discuss their misunderstandings and work toward a healthier approach for expressing their differences of opinion.

Coping with Loss

Jesus said good-bye in many ways. After a healing, he would say something like "Go in peace" (Mark 5:34) or "Go; your faith has made you well" (Mark 10:52). Sometimes, he would slip away without a word—often to get some quiet time. Jesus' most dramatic good-bye is recorded in Acts. Jesus gathered his disciples around him, said a few parting words, and ascended into heaven.

Like Jesus, spiritual leaders repeatedly say good-bye. Your responsibilities might include comforting the dying and presiding at funerals. In addition, you regularly bid farewell to colleagues and the people you serve as you or they move from post to post. This week you will consider your personal style of saying good-bye, your own losses, and how you can cope with the losses you experience in both your personal life and ministry.

Connecting with Yourself

1. Use your journal to record your answers to the following questions.
   - When you were a child, how did members of your family of origin typically say good-bye?
   - How do the people in your family of origin say good-bye now?
   - What is your "exit style" today? How does it differ in various contexts—with friends, family of origin, and people in your ministry setting?
   - In what ways has your preferred style of saying good-bye affected the way you receive or process the good-byes of others?

2.   Make a list of the most significant losses in your life. These can be the deaths of family or friends, the loss of a job, a community, good health, a project, a personal ambition, a friendship or other relationship, or anything else that you perceive to be a loss.
  • What life lessons have you learned as a result of experiencing these losses? (You may choose one loss and write about the life lessons it has taught you.)
    Add a check to each loss on your list that you are still actively grieving.
  • What tools or resources helped you to move beyond the losses you are no longer grieving?
  • In what ways could those tools and resources help you to process losses you continue to grieve?
3.   Using your journal, reflect on the following questions:
  • As you look at your life now, what do you most fear losing?
  • How does your religious faith help you to cope with those fears?

Connecting with a Partner

1.   Tell about some of the most beloved people from your ministry who have died.
  • What did these people mean to you?
  • What tools or resources helped you to cope with their loss while ministering with their families?
2.   Tell about some of the losses you have experienced in your ministry and how you have dealt with them. Examples might include members leaving your church, colleagues and staff moving away, leaving a parish and community, or the completion or closing of a program or ministry.

Connecting with God

Make a list of significant individuals in your life and ministry who have died. Reflect on the gifts they brought to your life. During your prayer time this week, thank God for giving you the opportunity to know each of these individuals.

Challenge

Though you may take time to say good-bye to people who have died, many of life's greatest losses are not marked by any ritual of farewell. This week, create a ritual to say good-bye to a loss that has not received a proper good-bye.

Pastor Bea planted a tree in her garden as a memorial to the baby she lost through miscarriage three years ago. Father Michael created a scrapbook of memories from his first parish. Jonathan, a youth director, gathered his graduating seniors together for a worship service that celebrated their time together and helped everyone to say good-bye.

Finding Community

Being a spiritual leader can be a lonely job. Some studies indicate that a sizable majority of clergy feel that they do not have a close friend. That may be surprising news to some of your parishioners; after all, spiritual leaders interact with a great number of people every day. Moreover, these interactions are often intimate and centered around life's ultimate questions. They take place over major life events—illness, death, birth, and marriage.

Even so, healthy boundaries dictate that spiritual leaders maintain some emotional distance from the people they serve. For example, when counseling someone who is experiencing marital problems, it would be inappropriate for you to share your own marital difficulties. In addition, a lack of time and energy prevents many spiritual leaders from finding and nurturing relationships outside of their ministry settings.

It's important that spiritual leaders develop a network of supportive relationships both inside and outside of their ministry setting. The size and scope of these relationships will vary depending on your own particular needs and situations. Single spiritual leaders may need to make more of an effort to discover a community beyond their ministry setting. This week you will look at your current support system, identify the places in which you need additional support, and create a plan for making new friends.

Connecting with Yourself

1. The list below compiles some of the many ways that we connect with other people. Using the list, write the names of the people in your support system who fit into each category (some people will fit into more than one category). Include friends, family, colleagues,

acquaintances, and supportive parishioners. Ideally, you will have people with whom you connect in each of these areas.

Common Connections
   a. emotional: connecting around feelings
   b. intellectual: connecting around ideas
   c. recreational: connecting around interests and hobbies such as quilting or making crafts, and other fun activities
   d. philosophical: connecting over an ideology or common cause such as political commitments
   e. work: connecting about one's job
   f. task: connecting by doing chores such as raking leaves or making household repairs.
   g. life-roles: connecting around one's stage or roles in life such as parenting, retiring, surviving cancer, or divorcing
   h. spiritual: connecting around one's faith and life's ultimate questions
   i. artistic: connecting around the arts—music, literature, movies, visual arts, and theater
   j. physical: connecting around doing activities such as running, swimming, yoga, dance, or volleyball
   k. specialized helpers: connecting around a set of issues or events that you have hired or asked others to help you with. This could include your physician, therapist, spiritual director, personal coach, mentor, or a support group.
   l. crisis: connecting to help one another in times of difficulty or crisis. These are people you can call to drive you to the hospital at 3:00 A.M.
   m. other

2. Looking at the list from exercise 1, use a highlighter to indicate any area in which you have *inadequate* support. People have differing needs for affiliation. You may define inadequate in any way that supports your needs for affiliation with others. If you appreciate face-to-face contact and all of your intellectual supporters are people you correspond with on the Internet, that may be inadequate to you.

   Do not forget to consider how much time you actually spend with the people named in each category. You might determine a category to be inadequate on the basis of the small amount of time you spend with those people and not because of a lack of persons with whom to connect. As you work with your partner, you will think about how you can make connections in these areas.

3. Just as it is important to connect with people in a variety of ways, it is essential for spiritual leaders to connect, in person, with people outside of their two major systems: religious institutions and family.

    Make a list of friends in your support system who fit the criteria below. You will be looking at this information with a partner.
    a. They are not people who relate to you primarily as a spiritual leader.
    b. They are not people with whom your common bond or primary connection is a religious institution or the place at which you work.
    c. They are not members of your immediate or extended family.
    d. They live within an hour's drive of your home.

4. Looking at all the work you have done thus far, make a support system or friendship wish list. Record the needs you have for friends in this way:
    *   I need to find people to connect with around (common connections).
    *   I need to find people to connect with (in my area, outside of the church, and so forth).
    *   I need to spend _____ hours with friends each week.
    When you have finished, decide which types of support you want to look for first.

Connecting with a Partner

1. Where would you rate yourself on a scale if 1 equaled "I am very lonely" and 10 equaled "I have more than enough friends"?
    *   In what ways have you found it possible to be friends with the people you serve in your ministry setting?
    *   In what ways has being friends with these people been difficult?
    *   What has the experience of making connections with people outside of your ministry setting been like for you?
2. Using your list of the types of support you want to look for, brainstorm ways that you can meet new people.
3. Develop a plan to meet new people and strengthen existing relationships in the next month.

Connecting with God

Pray for those people who are a part of your support system.

Challenge

Make an effort to meet new people and strengthen an existing relationship this week. For example, you might arrange to attend a gallery opening in order to meet other people who love art, and also arrange to go hiking with a current friend.

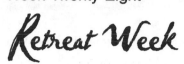

This retreat week provides another opportunity and a new setting from which to consider your relationships. Refer to the introduction for a description of the purpose and structure of a retreat week. As you create a retreat that is nurturing for you, you may want to use some of the following movies, books, and activities.

MOVIES AND VIDEO

The Big Chill
A group of college friends from the 1960s gathers 20 years after graduation to mourn the death of one of their classmates.

Cheers (the television series)
This situation comedy set in a bar in Boston explores the nature of community.

Fried Green Tomatoes
Based on Fannie Flagg's novel, this movie, set in the South, tells two separate stories. In the first, a woman discovers her own voice in her marriage and in the second, two women find lasting friendship.

Places in the Heart
Set during the depression in Texas, a widow discovers the power of the communities of both the living and the dead.

Sister Act
A lounge singer uses music to unite a convent community and its inner-city neighborhood.

Steel Magnolias
A community of women, who gather regularly in the town beauty shop, share the intimacies of their daily lives.

BOOKS

Fiction

Death Comes for the Archbishop by Willa Cather
In this novel, set in nineteenth century New Mexico, Father Jean Marie Latour confronts loneliness as he ministers to the native population.

Frog and Toad Together, Days with Frog and Toad, Frog and Toad Are Friends, and *Frog and Toad All Year* by Arnold Lobel
In these children's books, best friends Frog and Toad share their love for each other through many adventures.

The Giver by Lois Lowry
In a future society, a young boy must consider the importance of feelings and memories in relationships.

The Ladies Auxiliary by Tova Mirvis
A tight-knit community of orthodox Jews are challenged by the arrival of a new, more free-spirited member to their community.

Seedfolk by Paul Fleischman
An inner city community builds a garden and new relationships.

Vinegar Hill by A. Manette Ansay
In this multi-layered novel, a young woman struggles to negotiate her husband's family of origin when they move in with his parents.

Welcome to the Great Mysterious by Lorna Landvik
An actress takes time off to care for her nephew and rediscovers new truths about love and family.

Women of the Silk and *The Language of the Threads* by Gail Tsukiyama
A young woman, forced to leave her family and work in a silk factory in China, finds community in her new home.

Wilifred Gordon McDonald Partridge by Mem Fox
In this children's picture book, a small child helps an old woman rediscover her memory.

Nonfiction

Extraordinary Relationships by Roberta Gilbert
This book offers a helpful overview of family systems theory.

Family Ties That Bind by Dr. Ronald W. Richardson
Dr. Richardson provides information and questions for people wanting to further explore issues from their family of origin.

In the Shadow of God's Wings: Grace in the Midst of Depression by Susan Gregg-Schroeder
A pastor recounts her own struggle with depression.

Life Together by Dietrich Bonhoeffer
Bonhoeffer's classic exploration of Christian community provides a lasting vision of how Christians can live together.

Things Seen and Unseen: A Year Lived in Faith by Nora Gallagher
Gallagher, a laywoman, recounts a year in the life of her congregation—exploring the depths of Christian community.

ACTIVITIES

This might be a good time to explore some of the challenges that you did not have time to complete during the previous eight weeks. You may also want to repeat a challenge that was particularly useful to you. The following weekly challenges are best suited to a retreat: weeks eighteen, twenty-one, twenty-four, and twenty-five.

- Research your family's history on the Internet.
- Find a quiet place, be silent, and listen. What do you hear?
- Visit a cemetery.

- Go to a public place and watch people.
- Participate in an evening of group dancing or exercise.
- Arrange to spend time—either at home or away—with a close friend or family member.
- Reconnect with your immediate family or partner on a night away at a hotel or retreat center.
- Watch a movie that made you laugh the first time you saw it.
- Watch a movie that made you cry the first time you saw it. Have tissues available.
- Visit a comedy club or see a humorous play.
- Listen to recordings of inspirational speeches such as Martin Luther King Jr.'s "I Have a Dream."

Caring for Your Physical and Material Needs

Examining Your Attitude toward Your Appearance

You live in a culture that places great value on external appearances. In addition, you are exposed repeatedly to nearly unattainable standards of beauty. Attractive people sport washboard abs, straight, sparkling white teeth, and baby-smooth skin. The media bombards you with verbal and visual messages that remind you of the many ways in which you don't measure up.

Even though your values might tell you that there is more to life than the way you look, it is difficult to avoid the influence of cultural messages. Whether you obsessively attempt to pursue popular standards of beauty or give up all hope of attaining them, your attitudes about them and your appearance affect your general well being. This week's exercises will help you to gain a deeper appreciation for your body, blemishes and all, as you reflect on social and spiritual messages about beauty.

Connecting with Yourself

1. Take a day this week to pay attention to the messages you hear about both body and appearance. Make note of what you hear in the media, in your congregation, with friends and family, and inside your own head. You may want to record these messages in your journal. At the end of the day, review your list of messages and reflect on the following questions in your journal:
    *   In what ways does each message affect you?
    *   How would you respond to the message? Do you agree or disagree with it? If you disagree with it, how would you argue against it?

- Is there a pattern to the messages you hear?
- To which types of information about body or appearance are you most vulnerable?
- Do you hear anything helpful or inspiring?
- What are some of the messages about your body and appearance that you remember from your childhood and youth?

2. Draw an outline of yourself on a piece of poster board. Make a collage of words and pictures from magazines, newspapers, and your own pen that reflects the positive messages you would like to hold onto about your body and appearance. Your messages can be both about what your body can do and how it looks. You may want to include portions of the following Bible verses on your poster: Gen. 1:1–2:4; Ps. 139:1-18; Isa. 43:7; Isa. 44:2; Matt. 6:25-34; Rom. 12:1-2; 2 Cor. 4:7; 2 Cor. 5:17; or Eph. 2:10.

When you have finished creating your collage, put the poster in a place where it can remind you that you are God's wonderful creation.

Connecting with a Partner

1. What does your faith tradition say about the following: current cultural beliefs about beauty, the purpose of the body, clothing the body, and the relationship of body to spirit?
2. In your experiences as a spiritual leader, what messages have you received from your congregants about your body and its appearance? How have you responded to these messages? How have these messages affected you?
3. How have your beliefs about the body affected your attitudes and actions toward others?

Connecting with God

Take time this week to go outside and notice the beauty of God's creation. Look for beauty in places where you may not usually notice it.

Challenge

Stand in front of a mirror. You can choose any size mirror that feels comfortable. This exercise can be done fully clothed or unclothed, depending on your comfort level. Look at yourself and say, "God has created me. God loves me. I am beautiful. I love myself." Once you have mastered this first saying, speak the same message to the various parts of your body, both internal and external. For example, you might say, "God has created my lungs. God loves my lungs. They breathe beautifully. I love my lungs." Take extra time to focus on the parts of your body with which you are least comfortable or that are affected by chronic illness. If you are uncomfortable doing this exercise in front of a mirror, you can use it as a meditation. Picture in your mind each part of your body and silently repeat the words above (or something similar).

Eating Well

When Pastor Sam decided to visit every family in his congregation, he clustered his first seven visits on a Saturday. At the first home, he gladly welcomed the cup of coffee and the two large slices of apple strudel. At the second, he nibbled on a small slice of German chocolate cake. A piece of banana cream pie, three kinds of cookies, and two varieties of dessert bars later, Pastor Sam waddled home. As he collapsed on his couch and chewed on antacid tablets, he pondered how he could complete his next Saturday's visits without busting his belly and also not offending the gracious hosts in his parish.

Public events in churches and synagogues usually involve food. Spiritual leaders face an ongoing temptation to consume empty calories, and excessive amounts of stimulants such as caffeine and sugar. In addition, the schedule and pressures of ministry may prevent spiritual leaders from taking care of their nutritional needs. This week you will consider your attitudes and behaviors concerning food, and work on improving your daily diet.

Connecting with Yourself

1. Keep a food diary for the next three to four days. Write down everything you eat and drink, including water. Also record the times you consumed the food, the approximate size of your food portions, the situation, and how you were feeling at the time. You do not need to keep exact track of your calorie and nutrient content. The purpose of this exercise is to help you consider how you relate to food. A partial example follows.

7:00 A.M.   Regular coffee (two 8-ounce cups), oat cereal (1 cup) with whole milk (approximately 4 ounces), orange juice (6 ounces)
Breakfast with kids, feeling harried because of trying to get kids ready for school

10:00 A.M.   Coffee (two 8-ounce cups), donut (large with jelly inside)
Clergy meeting, feeling like I need an energy boost to keep going

1:00 P.M.   Fast-food burger (4 ounces with a slice of American cheese), French fries (8 ounces), cola (16 ounces)
Eaten in car on the way to the hospital, famished and rushed

2. Use your food diary to reflect on the following questions:
   - What patterns do you observe in the way you eat?
   - In what situations is eating most enjoyable for you? When is it least enjoyable for you?
   - When are you most likely to eat more than you need? When are you most likely to eat less than you need?
   - Do you have adequate time to prepare and eat your meals? If not, what prevents you from doing so?
   - How would you describe your general attitude toward food? Is it a blessing to be enjoyed or a curse to be thwarted? What factors affect your attitude toward food?
   - Do you use food or alcohol to fill emotional needs in your life? If so, in what ways?
   - Does your diet cause physical discomfort or health problems (examples include constipation, indigestion, high cholesterol, and diabetes)? If so, how often? In what ways?

3. The following checklist provides a general guideline for eating well based on standards advocated by the United States Department of Agriculture (www.usda.gov) and the American Dietetic Association (www.eatright.org). It is important for you to consult with your physician for guidance on your specific dietary needs. Check all of the statements that are true for you. If you are unsure about the amounts of food or other substances (such as fats or sodium) you are consuming, use your food diary and food labels as a guide.

   When you have finished, review any unchecked statements and consider how you could modify your diet to make those statements true. Make a list of eating goals for yourself.

_____ I drink eight 8-ounce glasses of water each day.

I consume sweets sparingly.

_____ I consume no more than 200–300 milligrams of caffeine each day (two 5-ounce cups of coffee).

_____ I consume no more than 2,400 milligrams of sodium each day (one level teaspoon of salt equals 2,300 milligrams).

_____ Fewer than 30 percent of my daily calories come from fats.

_____ Less than 10 percent of my daily calories come from saturated fats.

_____ I consume no more than 300 milligrams of cholesterol daily.

_____ I consume 3,500 milligrams of potassium a day.

_____ If I consume alcohol, I do so in moderation, with meals, and I do not put myself or others at risk.

_____ On average I eat 2 to 3 servings each day of milk, yogurt, or cheese (1 serving equals 1 cup of milk or yogurt; 1 ½ ounces of natural cheese; or 2 ounces of processed cheese).

_____ On average I eat 2 to 3 servings each day of meat, poultry, fish, beans, eggs, or nuts (1 serving equals no more than 3 ounces of cooked lean meat, poultry, or fish; 1 ½ cups of cooked dry beans; 1 egg; or 2 tablespoons of peanut butter).

_____ On average I eat 3 to 5 servings of vegetables each day (1 serving equals 1 cup of raw leafy vegetables; ½ cup of other vegetables, cooked or chopped raw; or ¾ cup of vegetable juice).

_____ On average I eat 2 to 4 servings of fruits each day (1 serving equals 1 medium apple, banana, or orange; ½ cup of chopped, cooked, or canned fruit; or ¾ cup of fruit juice).

_____ On average I eat 6 to 11 servings of whole-grain bread, cereal, rice, or pasta (1 serving equals 1 slice of bread; 1 ounce of ready-to-eat cereal; or ½ cup of cooked cereal, rice, or pasta)

Connecting with a Partner

For this chapter's exercises, we encourage you to meet over a nutritious meal that you have prepared together. If it is not possible to cook together, choose a restaurant that serves nutritious meals and eat there.

1. How have the following sources influenced your attitudes about food and eating: your family of origin, friends, the people you live with, people in your ministry setting, the media, and health professionals?
2. Brainstorm ways that you can improve your eating habits. Consider the following areas:
    *   How to balance healthy eating with a busy schedule.
    *   Ideas and resources for quick, easy-to-prepare nutritious meals.
    *   Maintaining your dietary goals in professional situations.
3. Share some of your favorite table graces.

Connecting with God

Take time to say a prayer of gratitude before each meal and snack you eat this week. If you are already in the habit of doing this, you might want to find a new table grace or recall one from your childhood.

Challenge

Review your checklist and goals from exercise 3 in Connecting with Yourself. Using this information as a guide, make at least one dietary change that will improve your health. Pastor Betty replaced her customary diet soda with water. Pastor Myron began making a healthy bag lunch to bring with him on busy days, foregoing his daily stop at a fast-food restaurant. Rabbi Ruth brought a healthy snack to share with others in her colleague group each week.

Designing an Exercise Routine

After Pastor Sam had visited every member of his congregation, he stepped on his bathroom scale and discovered that he had gained 15 pounds. That very day he decided to begin a regular exercise program of walking and lifting weights. Always the overachiever, he enthusiastically walked six miles on the first day and five on the second. After each walk he faithfully did a regiment of weight lifting exercises recommended by a popular fitness magazine.

On the third day Pastor Sam woke with tender muscles, barely able to lift the bottle of ibuprofen. After much debate, he decided to take a well-deserved day off from his exercise routine. A month later, as he wiped the dust off the weights, Pastor Sam concluded that he was too busy to take time for exercise now. Maybe he would try again in a few months.

If the road to hell is paved with good intentions, it probably includes a few out-of-shape spiritual leaders vowing that that they will spend time on their treadmill "one of these days." This week you will examine your own attitude toward exercise and design an exercise routine that fits your needs. Even if you failed your high school gym class or may currently face physical challenges, exercise can be part of your daily life. Consult your physician before beginning any exercise program.

Connecting with Yourself

1. Using your journal, make a list of both your current formal (examples include a daily jog or yoga exercise) and informal (examples include climbing stairs or doing daily housework) exercise habits.

- List all the exercises you normally do in an average week and the amount of time you spend in each activity.
- Rank your current satisfaction with your exercise routine on a scale of 1 to 10 (1 = I feel like a total couch potato; 10 = I'm doing the best I can).
- Next, make a list of what you would like your exercise habits to include one year from now. List both formal and informal activities.
- When you have finished, make a list of the attitudes, emotions, and situations that are currently preventing you from exercising as you like. What changes would you need to make to begin the habit of regular exercise?
- Make a list of the people who could support you in making these changes.

Sister Karen suffered from asthma and believed she was unable to exercise. After consulting with both her primary care physician and her allergist, she was able to obtain the medicine and information necessary to begin a moderate walking program. Pastor Mike rarely exercised, convinced he didn't have the time. He decided to combine some of his weekly reading with exercise, and now reads his theological journals while riding his stationary bicycle three times a week.

2. Design an exercise program that will fit with your lifestyle and physical needs and capabilities. Most experts consider a good exercise program to include stretching, 30 minutes of aerobic exercise three to five times a week, and strength training two to three times a week. As you create your personal program, be sure to:
   - Consult your primary care physician for both approval and suggestions.
   - Research possibilities for a variety of types of exercises. (See the appendix for books and Web sites to use in your search.)
   - Decide whether you want to exercise every day or several times a week. Frequency of exercise will depend on your current health and the types of activities you choose.
   - Set aside a specific time each day or week for exercise. Be sure to allow adequate time to "warm up" and "cool down" from your workout.
   - Start slowly to allow your body to adjust to the new routine. For example, you might want to plan to start with five minutes of daily exercise for the first week and then increase to 10 minutes for the second week, with the goal of continuing to increase your exercise time each week.

- Include a "restart" plan in case your exercise routine is interrupted.
- If time is a concern, you might use some of these ideas to build in small amounts of exercise throughout the day: park at the far end of the parking lot and walk, take the stairs at the hospital or in other public buildings, walk to work, do house and yard work.
- If exercise is unpleasant for you, you may want to combine it with another more enjoyable activity (examples include listening to music, watching a favorite video, reading a magazine, and calling a friend) or do it with a partner.
- If you are already exercising, you may want to try a new type of physical activity.

Connecting with a Partner

1. In what ways can you support each other in designing and following a personal exercise program?
2. What can you do to "restart" your exercise program when your regular routine is interrupted by illness, busy schedules, vacations, or other roadblocks?
3. In what ways can exercise be a spiritual activity?

Connecting with God

Combine prayer with an exercise or movement such as running, walking, yoga, stretching, dancing, or weightlifting. You might use a "breath prayer," saying the first part as you breathe in and the second as you breathe out. For example, you might pray, "Fill me/spirit" or "Guide me/Gracious God."

Challenge

Begin the exercise program you designed in Connecting with Yourself, exercise 2. Be patient. Don't expect immediate improvement in the way you look and feel. Remember that the benefits of exercise are long term. Envision yourself maintaining your exercise routine one year from now. It takes 21 days for an activity to become a habit. Make it a goal to continue every day for 21 days until your daily exercise becomes routine. Note that these 21 days may not be consecutive if your routine involves exercising three to four days a week.

Cultivating the Gift of Sleep

Humans need sleep to renew both their mental and physical health. The American Academy of Sleep Medicine (www.aasmnet.org) reports that more than 100 million Americans do not get a good night's sleep. A National Sleep Foundation (www.sleepfoundation.org) survey reveals that 40 million Americans suffer from sleep disorders. NSF statistics suggest that fatigue contributes to more than 100,000 highway crashes each year. Forty percent of Americans are so tired that sleepiness interferes with their daily tasks a few days a month.

As a spiritual leader working a "24/7" schedule, you may be among those who sacrifice a good night's sleep. This week you will reflect on what your current sleep habits and dreams tell you about your life and explore ways to improve your sleep hygiene.

Connecting With Yourself

1. Using your journal, reflect on the following questions:
    *   On average, how many hours a night do you sleep? (Eight hours is recommended.)
    *   How often do you nap and for what duration? (Researchers at the American Academy of Sleep Medicine suggest avoiding daytime naps. For those who need a nap, they recommend no more than one nap a day, lasting less than one hour, and taken before 3:00 P.M.)
    *   How would you describe the quality of your sleep?
    *   When are you least likely to sleep well?

- What events in your professional and personal life affect your sleep?
- What other factors (examples include foods, beverages, noise, and overall health) affect your sleep?

2. "Sleep hygiene" refers to both your sleeping environment and habits. Sleep researchers offer helpful tips for maintaining good sleep hygiene and improving one's chances for a restful night of sleep. (See the appendix for additional resources.)

Use the following checklist to assess your sleep environment and habits. Check each statement that is true for you. For each statement that you do not check, identify the steps that you would need to take to make that statement true.

_____ I keep regular hours, going to bed and getting up at approximately the same time each day.

_____ I avoid caffeine and alcohol within four to six hours of bedtime.

_____ I avoid nicotine close to bedtime and at night.

_____ I eat only light foods before bedtime (no double burritos with cheese!).

_____ I exercise regularly.

_____ I avoid strenuous exercise within four to six hours of bedtime.

_____ I have a bedtime ritual to help me let go of the worries of each day.

_____ I rarely take naps during the day.

_____ I use my bedroom only for sleep and sex.

_____ When I cannot sleep, I get out of bed and engage in quiet activities until I feel drowsy.

_____ I do not have a television in my bedroom.

_____ I sleep on a comfortable mattress.

_____ I sleep in an adequately sized bed.

_____ My pillows provide proper support.

_____ My bedding is safe and comfortable.

_____ Generally, the temperature in my bedroom is comfortable for sleeping.

_____ My bedroom is free of dust and clutter.

_____ My bedroom is dark and quiet enough for me to sleep.

_____ If I have a sleeping partner, that person generally does not disrupt me.

_____ If I have a sleeping partner, our bed is at least a queen size.

3. Many people have gained insights into their lives by taking time to record and reflect on their dreams. Some people believe that if you go to sleep with questions, your dreams can help you answer them. Using your journal, record your dreams each morning immediately upon waking. Do this for at least three consecutive nights. Use the following questions or some of your own for reflection:
   - What do you think your dreams are telling you about your waking life?
   - What recurring themes appear in your dreams, either in the past week or throughout your life? How are these themes significant for you?
   - What does each person in your dreams teach you about yourself?

Connecting with a Partner

1. In what ways is sleeping and the process of dreaming a spiritual activity for you?
2. How has being a spiritual leader affected both your sleeping habits and your dreams?
3. What resources or rituals do you find helpful when you are unable to sleep?

Connecting with God

Before going to bed each night this week, take time to read and meditate on some of the following scripture passages: Ps. 3:5; Ps. 4:8; Ps. 63:5-7; Ps. 91:1-5; Ps. 121; Prov. 3:24; or Matt. 11:28-30

Challenge

Improve your sleep hygiene using the checklist in Connecting with Yourself, exercise 2 as a guide. Generally, it is easier to change one's sleeping environment than one's sleeping habits, so you might want to start with simple modifications in your sleeping space. Sweet dreams!

Honoring the Gift of Sexuality

"What's sax?" our five-year-old son asked us.

We pretended we didn't hear his question.

It was seven in the evening and we had been playing a board game together in the family room. We had not been paying much attention to the seemingly harmless animated situation comedy on the television in the background. But few things escape our son's notice.

"What's sax?" our son repeated. "That word they said on TV." He meant "sex." But we didn't want him to know we knew what he meant.

"It's a musical instrument," we replied. We weren't ready for the "facts of life" conversation quite yet.

We live in a culture where sexual images and language seem to be omnipresent. Although most religious traditions regard sexuality as a gift to be honored, many spiritual leaders feel uncomfortable speaking and thinking about sexual matters. Yet, like everyone else, spiritual leaders are sexual beings. As difficult as it may be to address the issues surrounding your sexuality, doing so better enables you to express your sexuality in appropriate ways. This week you will consider your attitudes about sexuality, discuss how to make responsible choices, and decide how you will honor your own sexual needs.

Connecting with Yourself

1. In your journal reflect on the following questions:
   - How do you define sexuality?
   - What factors have affected your attitudes about sexuality? Your expression of your sexuality?

- What do you consider to be appropriate and inappropriate ways of expressing your sexuality?
- How has being a spiritual leader affected your attitudes about sexuality? In what ways has it affected your expression of your sexuality?

2. Everyone, whether in a relationship or single, experiences needs for intimacy, touch, and sexual expression. Using your journal, list your needs in each of these three areas.
   - In what ways are you able to meet these needs?
   - What changes would you need to make in order to be satisfied in each of these areas? Focus on solutions that you are able to accomplish and that are in keeping with your values.

   Pastor Marguarita, unhappily married but unwilling to divorce, made a commitment to make regular phone calls to her close female friends as a way of meeting her need for intimacy. Father Sean, who is celibate, receives regular massages and weekly haircuts to meet his need for touch. Pastor Pete, juggling a marriage, three small children, and a busy suburban parish, makes weekly dates with his wife for sexual intimacy.

Connecting with a Partner

1. What are your faith tradition's views about sexuality?
2. What is the relationship between sexuality and spirituality?
3. Spiritual leaders regularly confront situations in which they must make responsible sexual choices. What choices would you make in the following situations? What factors would affect the choices you make?
   As you consider each situation keep the following facts in mind:
   - Although you may not have control over your sexual feelings, you do have the ability to choose how you will respond to those feelings.
   - Because of the power inherent in the role of spiritual leaders, sexual relationships with your congregants are never appropriate.
   a. While working together on a weekend retreat, you experience sexual feelings toward a parishioner.
   b. While meeting alone with you, a congregant you have been counseling confesses to having sexual fantasies about you.
   c. A colleague repeatedly makes inappropriate sexual comments to you at meetings.

d. A colleague confides to you that she or he has been having a sexual relationship with a married parishioner.

e. A parishioner you are counseling about his or her sexuality asks you a question about your own sexual experiences.

Connecting with God

Read the Song of Solomon. In what ways does this book speak to your relationship with God? How are you God's "beloved"?

Challenge

Do something to take care of yourself sensually. If possible, arrange for this to be a weekly ritual. You might use some of the ideas you generated in Connecting with Yourself, exercise 2. Here are some additional suggestions: massage, bubble bath, haircut, facial, foot bath, pedicure, manicure, whirlpool, sauna.

Coping with Stress

Both Pastor Martha and Pastor Mary have a full schedule at their respective churches this Wednesday. After a fitful night of sleep, Pastor Martha wakes up later than she'd planned. She digs through the clothes in her closet in search of the one clean suit that fits. She gulps down three cups of coffee and a cookie as she hastily prepares her Bible study for the morning. After a mad search for her keys, she rushes off to work.

Pastor Mary rises early and starts her day with a morning prayer walk, taking time to stretch her body before and after. After a calming shower and leisurely breakfast of oatmeal and herbal tea, Mary dresses in one of the outfits she had set aside for work at the beginning of the week. As she leaves her home, she picks up her Bible study tote bag and her keys—both waiting for her by the door.

By the end of the day, both pastors have encountered more stressors. Pastor Martha, without many support or self-care systems in place, feels frazzled. She spends another restless night, tossing and turning. Pastor Mary, whose daily life includes many stress-relieving activities, sinks into bed feeling tired but content and sleeps well.

This week you will discover what you can do to better cope with the stress that is an inevitable part of every spiritual leader's life. You will identify the people, possessions, and poor systems that create added stress for you and work to better manage them. Finally, you will add stress-relieving activities to your daily life.

Connecting with Yourself

1. Certain relationships, possessions, and poor systems can irritate you and drain your energy. When you tolerate these situations, you allow them to cause unnecessary stress in your life. If you eliminate or minimize these irritants, you can significantly reduce the amount of stress in your life.

   Every two days, Pastor Jan and her husband run out of milk—something they usually discover at night, when their young daughter is in need of her bedtime bottle. Each week, Rabbi Deborah spends hours on the phone with a complaining cousin—time she needs to prepare her weekly teaching material. Every day, Father Geoffrey has to dig through a laundry basket of socks to find two that match.

   Using your computer or a separate sheet of paper (not your journal), make a list of the relationships, possessions, and poor systems that you are tolerating. Next to each item, make a note of how you could eliminate or minimize the problem. For example, Father Geoffrey made a commitment to match his socks each week while he watched his favorite television drama. He put the spares in a bag to be used as dust rags. Post your list in a prominent place. Pay attention to what irks you each day. Chances are, you will discover some hidden irritants. As you notice these irritants, jot them down. Try to come up with 50 items.

   As you have opportunity, review this list of irritants and try to think of ways to eliminate or minimize each of them. Most of them should have simple solutions.

2. Make a list of the activities that relieve stress or bring you joy or peace. List anything you can think of, even if you don't currently participate in the activity.

   When you have finished, mark a *D* next to those items you do daily, a *W* next to those that you do weekly, an *M* next to the ones you do monthly, and an *R* next to those you rarely do.

   Which of these activities would you like to add to your daily or monthly repertoire? How could you do this? Add at least one activity this week.

Connecting with a Partner

1. What about being a spiritual leader brings you joy?
2. What is stressful about being a spiritual leader?
3. What tools are most helpful to you in avoiding or coping with stress?
4. Choose a "stress-busting" activity to do together.

Connecting with God

Use guided meditation to help yourself cope with stress. Record the following words on an audio recorder and then play them back during your devotional time:

Close your eyes and pay attention to your breath [pause]. Picture yourself walking to a favorite place [pause]. When you arrive at the place you love, look around at the beauty that surrounds you. Take a deep breath. Thank God for the gift of what you see.

Find a comfortable place to sit down. As you are sitting and admiring the view, one of God's messengers approaches you. He or she carries a large burlap bag. The messenger says, "This bag is for your worries. Place your worries into the bag, one by one. As you put each worry into the bag, feel a sense of release [pause]." "Is that everything?" asks the messenger. You place your final worries in the bag.

The messenger says, "I will send these to God to be lovingly cared for. Be at peace."

The messenger ties the bag and hurls it in the air. It becomes a dove and flies away. Take a deep breath. Bid farewell to the messenger.

Take one last moment to admire the beauty of your favorite place. Slowly walk away and open your eyes.

Challenge

Consult your list of relationships, possessions, and systems that you are tolerating from Connecting with Yourself, exercise 1. Eliminate or minimize as many as you can. Start with the most simple. If some of the irritants involve other people, enlist them in discovering a solution. Rabbi Deborah sat down with the cousin whose complaining was irritating her. They agreed to meet once a week for coffee instead of making daily phone calls and to restrict their "complaining time" to five minutes each.

Connecting with Health Care Professionals

Father Leo's parishioners appreciate his concern for their health. He visits them faithfully in the hospital and at home. He refers the people he counsels to therapists he trusts. And he regularly preaches to them about how caring for their bodies is caring for God's creation.

When Father Leo began to feel unwell one spring, one of his parishioners said, "Father Leo, why don't you follow your own advice and take some time off to care for God's temple." Father Leo took a week of vacation to fit in all of the doctor appointments he had pushed aside for the past five years, including a check-up with both a therapist and a spiritual director.

Like Father Leo, many spiritual leaders encourage their parishioners to take good care of themselves while neglecting their own spiritual and physical health needs. This week you will attend to any basic healthcare needs that you have neglected.

Connecting with Yourself

1.   Using the following inventory, check each item that you have completed. Put a star next to the items that you have yet to complete. Try to make appointments for as many of these as possible. After each appointment, be sure you have your next appointment scheduled. On a calendar that provides dates for the next two years, record all of the appointments that you have made. Then, make a note of when you plan to make appointments for the following year.

_____ I have had my teeth cleaned by a dental professional in the last six months.

_____ I have had a complete physical examination by a medical professional in the last 12 months.

_____ If I am a woman, I have had a Pap smear and breast examination or mammogram in the last 12 months.

_____ I have had my eyes examined in the past two years.

_____ I have regularly scheduled meetings or annual consultations with a therapist.

_____ I meet regularly with a spiritual director.

_____ I have seen any specialists necessary for my health. (This might include a specific type of doctor or other specialist such as an allergist, chiropractor, dietician, or physical therapist).

Connecting with a Partner

1. What aspects of your physical, emotional, and spiritual self-care do you find it most difficult to attend to? What prevents you from attending to them?
2. Share the names of health care professionals you or others have found helpful. What have been your experiences with healthcare professionals?

Connecting with God

Say a prayer of gratitude for your body and each of its parts. As you pray for each part of your body, envision it functioning healthfully and to the glory of God.

Challenge

Do one thing (anything!), large or small, that will help to make you a more healthy person. Quit smoking, wear sunscreen, walk around the block once a day, start sleeping eight hours each night, replace one of your daily cups of coffee with a glass of water, skip your daily donut, floss, start taking calcium supplements (if it's alright with your doctor).

Managing Your Financial Resources

As we prepared to write this book, we asked spiritual leaders, "What advice about money do you wish you would have received in seminary?" Most spiritual leaders spoke about their congregational stewardship programs and what they wished they could have done better. Few of the spiritual leaders talked about managing their own financial resources.

Money is a difficult topic for many spiritual leaders to talk about. (For some, it is even more difficult than discussing sexuality.) Yet poorly managed money can cause tremendous pain and problems. This week you will consider whether you are spending and saving money in ways that are consistent with your spiritual values and in keeping with your financial means.

Connecting with Yourself

If you have a life partner with whom you share financial resources and material possessions, we recommend that you complete the exercises in this section with that person.

1. On a sheet of paper write, "What I (We) Earned." On this paper list all sources of household income from the past 12 months. This may include money received from salary, benefits, gifts, investments, or other sources. Next to each source list the approximate amount of income you received from it during the past 12 months.

On a second sheet of paper write, "What I (We) Spent." On this paper list the following categories: taxes, mortgage payments, automobile loan payments, other loan payments, insurance, automobile expenses, food, home furnishings and improvements, education, clothing, charitable contributions, recreation expenses, other expenses, and unaccounted for expenses. (You may want to list specific major items within some of these categories. For example, under recreation expenses you might include the items: vacation expenses, home entertainment expenses, and season football ticket expenses. You might divide the food category into money spent for dining out and money spent for eating at home. Personalize the categories in whatever way is most appropriate for you.) Approximate the amount of money you spent on each category or item during the past 12 months and record this amount next to the category or item.

On a third sheet of paper write, "What I (We) Saved." On this paper list any savings accounts, certificates of deposit, mutual funds, retirement plans, stocks, bonds, or other personal investments to which you contribute money. Next to each of these accounts, funds, or investments list the approximate amount of money that you contributed to it during the past 12 months.

After completing this exercise, review the information you have recorded and reflect on the following questions:
- How easy was this exercise for you to do?
- What factors contributed to it being easy or difficult?
- How comfortable did you feel doing this exercise?
- As you survey the approximate amount of money that you have received, spent, and saved over the past 12 months, what patterns do you observe?

2. In your journal, make a list of items, experiences, or activities on which you value spending your money. Your list might include buying clothes, renovating a home, taking a hiking trip, buying a daily latte, sponsoring a refugee family, purchasing gifts for your children, saving for your children's education, or subscribing to a concert series.

When you have finished, compare this list to your spending record in exercise 1 and reflect on the following questions:
- Are you spending enough money on the items, experiences, and activities that you value? If not, what is preventing you?
- Are you spending too much money on things that you do not value? Identify any areas in which you could reduce spending in order to have more money to spend in ways consistent with what you value.

3. Use the following checklist to evaluate your money habits. Check each statement that is true for you. For each statement that you do not

check, identify the steps you would need to take to make that statement true.

_____ I am satisfied with the amount of my annual income.

_____ I am satisfied with the amount of money I am saving toward retirement.

_____ I am satisfied with the amount of money I am saving toward large purchases.

_____ In the event of an emergency, I have enough money to support myself and those for whom I am responsible for six months.

_____ I am satisfied with the amount of money I give in charitable contributions.

_____ I spend my money in accordance with a budget or plan.

_____ For the most part, I spend my money in ways that are consistent with my values.

_____ I keep my financial records up to date.

_____ I am comfortable with the amount of debt that I have incurred.

_____ If I have a life partner, we regularly discuss financial matters.

_____ I pay my bills on time.

_____ I have adequate resources for receiving sound financial advice.

Connecting with a Partner

1. How has your faith tradition influenced your attitude towards money?
2. How has being a spiritual leader affected your attitude towards money? How has it affected your habits with money?
3. What aspects of money and finances do you find most confusing? Most interesting? Most anxiety producing?

Connecting with God

This week every time you handle money (in cash, check, or credit card form) offer a prayer of thanks to God for the gifts you have been given.

Challenge

Choose at least one of the items you did not check on the checklist about your spending habits (Connecting with Yourself, exercise 3). Begin taking the steps that you have determined you need to follow in order to make that statement true.

Pastor Annika and Pastor Miguel, a clergy couple, who rarely spoke about financial matters with one another, agreed to have a monthly discussion on the state of their finances. Catherine, a parish nurse who frequently could not account for how she spent much of her money, created a weekly budget plan and began spending her money in accordance with it.

Attending to Unfinished Financial Matters

Pastor Jack had been intending to call his insurance agent for quite awhile. He wasn't sure whether his home and valuables were adequately covered in case of a fire, flood, tornado, or other natural disaster. Most days he hardly gave this concern any thought. But at least twice a month he would wake at three in the morning, wide-eyed and worried, concerned that he still hadn't gotten around to making that call. "Tomorrow, I'll do it," he would think.

This week you will take on many of the tasks that can languish on to-do lists indefinitely. These are the jobs that may cause you to cringe. They put before you your own mortality and the possibility of accidents and illnesses. At the very least, they force you to ask bottom-line questions of bureaucracies. Yet attending to these tasks will no doubt contribute to your peace of mind.

Begin and end the week by treating yourself well. Eat, rest a bit, and then get to it! If you have a life partner with whom you share financial resources and material possessions, we recommend that you complete the exercises in this section with that person.

Connecting with Yourself

1. Using the following inventory, check each statement that is true for you. Put a star next to the statements that are not true. Attend to the matters you have starred as soon as possible.

    _____ I have a will that is signed, current, and accessible.

    _____ If I have children, I have selected guardians and made the appropriate arrangements with the guardians and in my will.

_____ I have made a living will.

_____ I have granted power-of-attorney to someone I trust in case I am incapacitated.

_____ I have granted power-of-attorney for healthcare to someone I trust in case I am incapacitated.

_____ I have adequate health insurance coverage.

_____ I have adequate disability insurance coverage.

_____ I have adequate life insurance coverage.

_____ My life partner and children have adequate health, disability, and life insurance coverage.

_____ If appropriate, I have started and regularly contribute to a fund to provide for my children's future educational needs.

_____ I have adequate homeowner's or renter's insurance coverage.

_____ I have adequate auto insurance coverage.

_____ I have adequately insured all other valuables in my possession.

_____ I am receiving the best rates possible for local and long distance phone service.

_____ I am receiving the best rates possible for my cell phone.

_____ I am satisfied with the rate of interest I pay on all of my loans and credit card debt.

_____ I have a safety deposit box for important papers.

_____ I have a tax consultant whom I trust.

_____ I have a financial planner whom I trust.

_____ I have an effective system for saving receipts and other important documents for tax purposes.

_____ I save my credit card and ATM receipts and check them against bills and statements each month.

_____ I am satisfied with the rates and services I currently receive from my financial institution.

_____ I have made a financial plan to provide for my funeral and have left a copy of this with a trusted friend.

Connecting with a Partner

1. What obstacles do you face in completing the items on the list from Connecting with Yourself?

2. In what ways can you support each other in completing the items on this list?

Connecting with God

Each day, visualize yourself doing the tasks on the list above. Envision God's presence with you, helping you to complete each step of the process. Express your gratitude to God for providing guidance and help.

Challenge

Save your change and any other extra money you can while completing the exercises for this chapter. When you have completed every item on the list, use the money to celebrate in some way that is appropriate for you.

Organizing Your Living Space

Pastor Shirley knew she had frankincense and myrrh somewhere in her house. She wanted to use it in her children's sermon the next morning. She dug through closets and cupboards, drawers and boxes—and came up empty. "If only I were more organized," she thought.

Those were the same words that Rabbi Stacey muttered as she dug through the papers on her dining room table, searching for the permission slip for her son's school trip to the zoo. She hoped she would find it in time for school that morning.

"It's time to buy more stamps," shouted Pastor Harry.

His wife, Pastor Shelly, yelled from the kitchen, "We just bought stamps!"

"Where are they?" asked Harry.

"Who knows?" responded his wife.

Even the most organized people have some clutter in their lives. This week you will take time to order the space in which you live. If you share your living space with others, we recommend that you complete the exercises in this section with them.

Connecting with Yourself

1. Reflect on the following questions in your journal for each room of your living space. If you live in a loft or studio apartment, do this exercise for each area of your living space.
   - What do you love about this space?
   - What about this space frustrates you? Create a list of everything about your space that annoys you. Examples might include piles of

mail scattered about the house or clothes spilling over the laundry hamper.

- What are the "stuff holes" in this space—the places where you leave all of the things you don't want to deal with in the present moment?
- Ideally, what would you like this space to look like? (You might want to draw a floor plan.)
- What systems do you need to set up to make this happen? For example, you may need to create a specific place for your children to leave their important papers each day after school, or you may need to designate a shelf for library books and rented video tapes.

2. Referring to your analysis of your living spaces, organize one room at a time using the following steps. If the room contains storage areas, such as closets or bookshelves, concentrate on these areas of the room one at a time.

Sort and Review

Gather two boxes and a laundry basket. Label one box "donate" and the other "save." The basket is for items that belong in other parts of your home.

Review all of the items in the room or storage area. Ask yourself:

- Is this something I have used in the last year?
- Is this something I like?
- Is this something that has meaning to me?

If the object does not match any of these criteria, it is probably something you can place in the "donate" box. If you find that hard to do, yet do not see a purpose for the object in daily life, place it in the "save" box. When the box is full, seal it, and place it in a storage area. In six months, if you have not opened the box, donate it to charity.

Sort the remaining items by type and the season when you use them. For example, if you are organizing a closet, you would group all of the sweaters together.

Create Order

Looking at the piles of items, ask yourself:

- How can I order these items so that they are easily accessible? (Make sure to create an organizational system that fits with your habits.

If you tend to open and sort your mail at the kitchen table, the kitchen might be a good place to create a mail filing system. If you are a regular baker, make sure your baking supplies are easy to access. If you rarely bake, you might be able to store those supplies in the basement.)

- What storage containers or organizing devices (examples include shelves, plastic containers, and bins) do I need to make this area organized and functional?

Clean anything that needs to be cleaned, purchase the necessary items, put away the piles of stuff, and admire your work!

Before moving onto the next room or area, take time to put away all of the items in the basket.

Connecting with a Partner

1. Visit each other's homes. What does the space tell you about the person who lives here? What about this space is incongruent with the person who lives here?
2. Discuss ways that you can support each other as you complete this week's tasks.

Connecting with God

Ask God to bless each item you get rid of. Ask God to ensure that it ends up in a place where people will use it, cherish it, and find it meaningful.

Challenge

The exercises this week have focused on making your living space more functional. As a challenge, do one thing that will add beauty to your living space. Examples include painting a wall, hanging a curtain, purchasing a plant, hanging a piece of art, arranging some of your treasured possessions on a side table or mantle, and creating a centerpiece with objects from nature.

Maintaining a Safe Living Environment

Has it been four years since you checked the batteries in your fire alarm? Have you driven 12,000 miles since you last changed your oil? Did the aspirin in your medicine cabinet expire 10 years ago? Your situation may not be this extreme, but no doubt there are some safety issues that need your attention. This week you will evaluate the safety of your home, yard, and car and take care of any safety problems that exist. If you share your living space or transportation with others, we recommend that you complete the exercises in this section with them.

Connecting with Yourself

Using the following inventory, check each item that is true for you. Put a star next to the items that are not true. Attend to the matters you have starred as soon as possible.

_____ I have an adequate number of working smoke detectors in my home.

_____ I have changed the batteries in my smoke detectors in the last six months.

_____ I have an adequate number of working carbon monoxide detectors in my home.

_____ In case of fire, I have planned and practiced an escape route from my home for myself and my family.

_____ I have an adequate number of working fire extinguishers in my home, including one in the kitchen.

_____ I have emergency telephone numbers posted in a prominent place in my home.

_____ I carry a working cellular telephone or similar communication device while traveling in my car.

_____ My family and I have planned and discussed what to do in case of threatening weather.

_____ I have an adequately stocked emergency medical kit in my home.

_____ I have an adequately stocked emergency storm kit in my home.

_____ I have an adequately stocked emergency kit in my car.

_____ I have eliminated any fire or safety hazards from my home.

_____ If I have young children, I have taken adequate measures to ensure their safety in my home, yard, and car. (See the appendix for helpful Web sites.)

_____ I keep my car regularly maintained.

_____ My home has been tested for the presence of radon.

_____ If I have young children or animals, I have had my home tested for the presence of lead paint.

_____ I keep my home free of mold and excess dust.

_____ I have an adequate supply of any necessary medicine, which I check regularly to make sure it has not expired. It is stored in a safe place, out of the reach of children and pets.

_____ Other. (Use this space for any task that is unfinished or incomplete in your home, yard, or car.)

Connecting with a Partner

1. How can you support each other in completing the tasks on the list above?

Connecting with God

With your partner and other trusted friends and family, arrange to have a blessing ceremony for your home and car. You may choose to bring candles, incense, and music to enhance your ceremony. The section titled "Blessings" in the appendix includes resources that can help you.

Challenge

Create a system to support the regular completion of one of the tasks on the checklist above. If you have time, you may choose to create systems for more than one task. This might include creating a plan for weekly house cleaning, setting dates for regular car maintenance, or setting up a system for checking and refilling your emergency equipment.

Week Forty

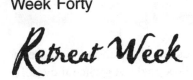
Retreat Week

This retreat week provides another opportunity and a new setting from which to consider your physical and material needs. Refer to the introduction for a description of the purpose and structure of a retreat week. As you create a retreat that is nurturing for you, you may want to use some of the following movies, books, and activities.

MOVIES AND VIDEO

Affluenza and *Escape from Affluenza*
Affluenza is an hour-long PBS special about the American problems of materialism and over-consumption. *Escape from Affluenza* is the solution-focused sequel. The PBS Web site, www.pbs.org, offers a study guide for viewers.

Babette's Feast
A French woman prepares an extravagant feast for two pious sisters and their friends, demonstrating that pleasure is one of God's great gifts.

Enchanted April
Four British women escape their dreary London lives for a month at a castle in Italy, finding themselves once again enchanted with life.

Healing and the Mind (Bill Moyers)
This five volume video series examines the connections between mind and body in the healing process, exploring Eastern medical practices.

Keeping the Faith
A Catholic priest and a Jewish rabbi, friends since childhood, explore the relationship between their personal and professional lives when they fall in love with the same woman.

Like Water for Chocolate
When a woman's family denies her the opportunity to marry her true love, she pours her passion into her cooking. This film is based on the book of the same name by Laura Esquivel.

Madame Blueberry
In this VeggieTales (TM) video, Madame Blueberry suffers the consequences of greed and learns to be thankful.

Spontaneous Healing (Andrew Weil)
Physician and popular author Andrew Weil offers his philosophy on the body's ability to heal itself.

BOOKS

Fiction

A Gracious Plenty by Sheri Reynolds
Finch Nobles, badly burned as a child and now living alone, moves easily between the world of the dead and the world of the living.

A Ring of Endless Light by Madeleine L'Engle
In this young adult novel, Vicky Austin must come to terms with the dying of her beloved grandfather, a new relationship, and a spiritual encounter with the dolphins.

A Reckoning by May Sarton
Laura Spelmen receives a terminal cancer diagnosis and uses her remaining time to let go of that which is not essential and focus on the important connections in her life.

Altar Music by Christin Lore Weber
Explore with three generations of Minnesota women the connections between faith, artistic passion, and sexuality.

The Green Mile by Stephen King
A man sentenced to death row reveals that his God-given powers are for healing, not killing.

Mariette in Ecstasy by Ron Hansen
A passionately devout young woman, a postulant in a New York convent in 1906, appears to experience ecstatic encounters with the divine.

The Napping House by Audrey and Don Wood
The gentle rhythm of this playful children's picture book might lull you to sleep.

Oh, Were They Ever Happy by Peter Spier
In this children's picture book, three children decide to paint the house while their parents are out for the day. The hilarious illustrations convey the passion that goes into the project as well as the parents'xfv reaction to the paint job.

Souls and Bodies by David Lodge
Lodge follows a group of friends from their college days until middle adulthood, marking their struggle to discover how to weave together their Catholic faith, their sexuality, and their daily lives.

Nonfiction

Feasting with God: Adventures in Table Spirituality by Holly Whitcomb
Whitcomb provides themes, discussion questions, and recipes for feasts. Themes include a global potluck, a winter picnic, and a comfort feast.

The Kitchen Congregation by Nora Seton
Seton recalls the stories and the people populating her mother's kitchen.

Kitchen Table Wisdom by Rachel Naomi Remen
Remen, a physician, reminds the reader that sharing stories "around the kitchen table" can bring hope and healing.

Limbo by A. Manette Ansay
Ansay, a novelist, documents her faith struggles in the midst of fighting a mysterious illness that ended her piano career in her early twenties.

The Not So Big House by Sarah Susanka
This book contains photos, floor plans, and text illustrating the movement toward "not so big" homes that use space more efficiently.

Simplify Your Life: 100 Ways to Slow Down and Enjoy Things That Really Matter by Elaine St. James
A small book of big ideas for creating a more simple lifestyle.

Spiritual Nightlights: Meditations for the Middle of the Night by Linda K. DeVries
DeVries, a recovering insomniac, offers meditations, prayers, and suggestions for those who suffer from sleep disorders.

ACTIVITIES

This might be a good time to explore some of the challenges that you did not have time to complete during the previous eleven weeks. You may also want to repeat a challenge that was particularly useful to you. The following weekly challenges are best suited to a retreat: twenty-nine, thirty, thirty-one, thirty-three, thirty-four, and thirty-five.

- Using the book, *Feasting with God*, create a meaningful feast with friends or family.
- Take a day for fasting and prayer.
- Spend a day or weekend at a spa.
- Create your own spa evening at home. You may want to invite friends to share the event with you. (Use Spa magazine or another popular magazine as a guide.)
- Take a weekend to rest and relax, doing only those activities that relieve stress and promote well-being.
- Take a weekend or an evening break for sleeping at a hotel or retreat center. Make sure your sleeping area is comfortable. Turn off the television, radio, phones, and pagers.
- Take mini retreats throughout your day to "stimulate your senses." Burn a scented candle. Use scented lotion. Sip a hot cup of herbal tea. Bake chocolate brownies or apple pie. Go to a pet store or the humane society and cuddle a furry animal. Take in a concert or play one of your favorite compact discs. Visit an art museum or take a nature walk.

- Take a romantic getaway with your life partner.
- Play Monopoly® with family or friends as a way to think about your attitudes toward money.
- Read and reflect on Jesus' parables about money.
- Read the Gospel of Luke and ponder the question, "What did Jesus say about wealth?"
- Read and reflect on any or all of the 10 meals mentioned in the Gospel of Luke. They are recorded in Luke 5:29-39; 7:36-50; 9:10-17; 10:38-41; 11:37-52; 14:1-24; 19:1-27; 22:7-38; 24:28-32; 24:36-49.
- On the Internet take a tour of cities you would like to live in. Be sure to take virtual tours of the homes in the area.
- Design your ideal home.
- Try a physical activity you have never tried before.
- Create your own fantasy camp—an experience in which you can pretend to be a professional athlete, a musician, or fulfill another lifelong dream. Consider a baseball, cheerleading, track, music, or cooking camp. Let your imagination run wild and then invite your friends and an expert trainer. (Or research and attend a camp run by others.)
- Invite friends to a sleepover. Include sensual treats like a toasty warm fire, s'mores, popcorn, and scary stories.

Caring for Your Spiritual and Intellectual Needs

Experiencing God's Grace

Pastor Maria couldn't have planned it had she tried. She had been rushing around all day, attending to her many duties as a spiritual leader and mother. After two difficult visits with parishioners at the hospital, she picked up her daughter from school. With just a few minutes to spare she had to drop off her daughter for dance lessons and drive across town to the church for a meeting.

As Pastor Maria sped along the freeway, she reflected on her hospital visits, her upcoming meeting, and what she might preach about on Sunday. Her daughter sat sullenly in the back of the car, unnoticed by her preoccupied mother. Suddenly ahead on the freeway, Pastor Maria saw cars lined up for miles. She slowed down and then stopped, where she and her daughter waited for 45 minutes, missing the dance lesson and the meeting.

"So, how are you?" she asked her daughter, whose sullen expression she noticed for the first time.

And that's when it happened. They talked. For the first time in weeks. About school and work and life and God and all sorts of other subjects. Later, Pastor Maria recognized it as a moment of grace, an unexpected gift from God, which lifted her spirits in the midst of an otherwise hectic day.

Though much self-care depends on you, as a spiritual leader you know that ultimately all of life is God's gift. God strengthens and sustains you in both familiar and surprising ways. This week you will take time to reflect on moments of grace in your life and how God works through them to nurture you.

Connecting with Yourself

1. In your journal, reflect on the following questions:
    *   How has God strengthened you in times of weakness?
    *   When have you experienced God's grace through the actions or words of others?
    *   In which places have you experienced God's grace?
    *   When have you experienced God's grace through literature, music, or art?
    *   How has God answered your prayers?
    *   What miracles or wonders have you witnessed?
    *   When have you experienced an otherworldly peace?
    *   When have you felt or known that you are unconditionally loved by God?
    *   What are some of the unexpected ways you have experienced God's grace?
    *   What prevents you from experiencing God's grace?
2. After reflecting on the questions above, compile a list of ways that you experience God's grace. Post this list in a prominent place and refer to it throughout the week as a reminder of God's blessing.
3. Interview people about their spiritual journeys. You might choose colleagues, mentors, congregants, friends, or family. Ask them to describe their most meaningful spiritual experiences.

Connecting with a Partner

1. How has God strengthened and sustained you throughout your ministry?
2. Describe a moment from your ministry that was a powerful spiritual experience.
3. Describe one of your most meaningful public worship experiences.
4. What are your favorite scripture passages? Why?

Connecting with God

As a creative meditation exercise, read and reflect on one or more scripture passages that describe a human encounter with the divine. Examples include Jacob wrestling a stranger (Gen. 32:22-32), Moses and the burning bush

(Exod. 3:1–4:17), Samuel's vision (1 Sam. 3:1-15), Isaiah's epiphany (Isa. 6:1-13), and Mary and Gabriel (Luke 1:26-38).

After reading the passage several times, close your eyes and imagine what the experience must have been like for the human participants. What might they have seen, heard, smelled, felt, or tasted? What emotions might they have experienced? What thoughts might have passed through their minds? What would you have done in their situation? What does this story tell you about God?

Challenge

When do you overlook God's moments of grace? How might you pay more attention to what God is doing in the world? In some Jewish traditions people make a practice of thanking God for each blessing that they see throughout the day. For example, one might wake to a beautiful sunrise and pray, "Blessed are you, O God, Ruler of the Universe, who blesses my life with the gifts of light and warmth."

This week, take a day to pay attention to the ways that God blesses you in the events, people, and places of your life. If you wish, make your own prayer of blessing each time you experience a moment of grace. You may want to write about these experiences at the end of the day.

Attending to Your Own Spiritual Life

One of our parishioners once said to us, "You spiritual leaders have the perfect job. You get to think about God all day."

We wish it were so! Just as you might suppose that professional athletes are in excellent physical condition, many people assume that spiritual leaders have perfect spiritual lives. As you know, this is not always the case. Many spiritual leaders are like hosts who run around catering to the needs of their guests. They make sure that everyone else is fed, even while they may themselves be hungry.

As a spiritual leader you pray for others. You counsel, encourage, serve, and care for them. Yet unless you take time to care for your own spiritual needs, you damage your ability to care for others. This week you will examine and seek to improve your own spiritual practices. You will consider how attending to your own spiritual life can improve your effectiveness as a spiritual leader.

Connecting with Yourself

1. In your journal reflect on the following questions:
   - Before you became a spiritual leader, what were your expectations in regard to how you would experience and practice your spirituality?
   - How has your relationship with God changed in the time you have been a spiritual leader?
   - In what ways has being a spiritual leader affected your personal spiritual practice? What has surprised you? What has challenged you?

2. Imagine yourself doing something wonderfully spiritual. What would that be?

3. Look at the list that follows and place a checkmark next to the statements that reflect your current situation. Do not place a checkmark by any practice that you engage in only in your role as a spiritual leader. (For example, if the only small group you participate in is at the congregation you lead, do not include that here.) Read the list a second time and use a highlighter to note the statements that reflect spiritual practices you currently desire to have in your life.

_____ I pray at a regular time each day.

_____ I pray spontaneously throughout the day.

_____ I use written prayers and devotions to guide my spiritual time.

_____ I read theological books to guide my spiritual time.

_____ I read the Bible daily for my own spiritual growth.

_____ I regularly meet with another person for prayer, study, or spiritual support.

_____ I regularly meet with a small group for prayer, study, or spiritual support (examples include a recovery group, a Bible study group, or a support group).

_____ I regularly meet in a community (for which I am not the leader) for spiritual prayer, worship, study, or support.

_____ I use meditation as a tool during my spiritual time.

_____ I use a rosary or prayer beads as a tool during my spiritual time.

_____ I walk the labyrinth as a regular part of my spiritual life.

_____ I use dance, yoga, walking, or other physical activity as a part of my spiritual practice.

_____ I make a regular retreat to care for my spiritual health.

_____ I have a spiritual director.

_____ I have a friend or mentor with whom I speak about spirituality.

_____ I use journaling as a tool for spiritual growth.

_____ I use icons or other objects that help me to connect with God (examples include a Zen garden, a fountain, or a rock) during my prayer or meditation time.

_____ I have icons or other objects that help me to connect with God in a special place to remind me of God's presence in my life.

_____ I use chanting or singing as a part of my spiritual practice.

_____ I use recorded music as a part of my spiritual practice.

_____ I use fasting as a part of my spiritual practice.

_____ I have a Web site that I connect to for guidance in my daily spiritual time.

_____ I participate in an online community for spiritual support.

_____ I use the Internet as a tool for finding new resources for my spiritual journey.

_____ I go regularly to a place that is sacred to me.

_____ I have a sacred space within my home or office.

_____ I participate in a regular activity that I consider to be a spiritual practice (examples include fishing, baking bread, woodworking, and gardening).

_____ I participate in a volunteer activity that I consider to be a spiritual practice (examples include teaching literacy, building homes, rocking newborns, and cooking for the homeless).

_____ Other statements that either define my current spiritual practices or reflect what I long for:

Connecting with a Partner

1. In what ways does God nurture you through your regular ministry tasks?
2. What personal spiritual practices are helpful to you?
3. How does attending to your own spiritual needs affect your ministry as a spiritual leader?

Connecting with God

Do one or both of the following:
- Create or find a sacred space that is meaningful to you and use it in your prayer time this week.
- Find an icon or sacred object that you can use during your prayer time or at other moments in the day.

Challenge

Choose at least one spiritual practice (from the list above or from your own list of yearnings) and take the steps necessary to establish it in your life.

Mining Sources of Wisdom

We have heard that an average American living today takes in more information in a month than people one hundred years ago received in a lifetime. As a spiritual leader you need to stay abreast of current events, social trends, and the latest ideas. Yet all this information can be overwhelming. In the midst of e-mail, Web sites, periodicals, opinionated friends and parishioners, and television newscasts, where do you turn for real wisdom you can use?

Discovering wisdom in the information age is like panning for gold. You must sift through a lot of worthless material in order to attain the treasured nuggets you seek. Yet wisdom can also be discovered in untapped and sometimes unexpected sources. This week you will identify your most helpful sources of wisdom and renew your commitment to them.

Connecting with Yourself

1. We may miss much of the wisdom that comes to us in ordinary circumstances because we are not paying attention. Throughout the next day, seek to gain as many pieces of wisdom as you can in the midst of living your daily life. This might include important nuggets of information, wise sayings, spiritual truths, and new perspectives on life. The wisdom can come from your spouse, friends, children, strangers, parishioners, books, media, and even your own thoughts. At the end of the day, reflect on the following questions in your journal:
    *   What pieces of wisdom did you collect?
    *   How did the goal of seeking wisdom change the way you experienced the events of your daily life today?

- What did you learn from this experience that you might apply to your life every day?

2. Make a list of the sources of wisdom that you have valued throughout the various stages of your life (childhood, adolescence, college, graduate school, first call, as a single person, as a parent of young children, and so forth). This might include favorite books, special places, activities, and persons.

    Place a checkmark next to those items on the list that you are currently consulting as sources of wisdom.

    Circle the items that are not current sources of wisdom and that you would like to utilize in your life today. What steps do you need to take to reconnect with these sources of wisdom?

    Take steps to reconnect with one source of wisdom this week. Here are some examples. Pastor Iyanla discovered that reading fiction inspired and enlightened her. She decided to replace two hours of television viewing each week with reading. Sister Mary Jo decided to reconnect with an aunt who had taught her how to garden and can vegetables in her childhood. Father Tim remembered gaining insight on the long walks he took during his days at seminary and decided to walk 30 minutes each day in a local park.

Connecting with a Partner

1. At the end of interviews, the film critic Gene Siskel used to ask, "What do you know for sure?" Take turns completing the sentence "I know for sure that . . ." until you run out of certainties. Do not comment on what you are saying during the exercise. When you have finished, reflect on the following questions:
    - What does this exercise tell you about sources of wisdom and knowledge?
    - How has "what you know for sure" changed throughout your life?
    - How has "what you know for sure" changed during the time you have worked as a spiritual leader?
2. What are the most important things you have learned? How does having this knowledge affect your life and future plans?
3. In what ways has mentoring others instructed you about life?

Connecting with God

In the Hebrew Bible, wisdom is personified (see Prov. 8–9) as "Lady Wisdom." Write a dialogue between yourself and Lady Wisdom each day this week. Ask her questions, talk to her about your life, explore your relationship with God. Write both your questions and her responses. As you do so, do not stop to think about what you might write—simply record whatever comes into your head.

Challenge

In what part of your life would a mentor be helpful to you? Begin to pray and think about someone who could mentor you. If you think of someone, approach that person and work out a plan to develop a mentoring relationship.

Pastor Miguel, recently diagnosed with diabetes, chose a man who also had diabetes and who was living a full life with the disease, to guide him toward a healthier lifestyle. Sister Anna had always admired the quilted art of a colleague in ministry. She asked the colleague to mentor her in developing her own quilting skills. Pastor James, a psychotherapist as well as a member of the clergy, spent an hour a week with another psychotherapist to review current academic studies and practical cases.

New Tools and Topics in Ministry

In his book, *Gravity and Grace*, theologian and seminary professor Joseph Sittler laments the fact that many spiritual leaders reach their highest level of theological knowledge during their senior year in seminary. In his experience, many spiritual leaders never read another book on biblical studies, faith history, or theology during their ministry.

Futurist Alvin Toffler once said, "The illiterate of the 21st century will not be those who cannot read or write but those who cannot learn, unlearn, and relearn." Continuous lifelong learning is a critical element of self-care. In order to remain physically and mentally healthy, spiritual leaders need to incorporate new ideas into both their personal and professional lives. This week you will take inventory of your ministry and create a learning plan for the next year.

Connecting with Yourself

1. As a spiritual leader, what do you need to "learn, unlearn, and relearn"? Make three columns on a page in your journal. From left to right label them, "learn," "unlearn," and "relearn." Jot down everything that comes to mind for each of the three categories. Reflect on these questions:
   - What do your lists tell you about how you might approach your ministry differently?
   - What do your lists tell you about the topics you need to pursue in continuing education?
   - What do your lists tell you about the type of continuing education you need to pursue?

2. Design a continuing education program that meets your needs. Include a list of specific learning goals, a plan of action, and a timeline for completing your goals. Try to use a learning method that fits with your style of learning. (Visual learners learn through seeing; auditory learners learn through listening; and tactile/kinesthetic learners learn by moving, doing, and touching.) Consider creating unique learning opportunities instead of simply taking part in the programs offered by existing institutions. Here are some ideas to get you started:

   - Spend an internship at a congregation that is doing the type of ministry you seek to learn. You could discover such congregations through an Internet search or by interviewing colleagues in ministry.
   - Volunteer to be a pastor-in-residence at a seminary or college.
   - Shadow professionals in other fields. How might learning about what a manager, CEO, sales professional, or physician does change your approach to your job?
   - Shadow several spiritual leaders over the course of a year.
   - Create a learning retreat with some of your colleagues.
   - Do original research in a field that interests you (for example, to study youth, watch MTV or visit their local hangouts).
   - Create a reading list to accompany your learning activity.
   - Attend conferences of parallel professions (such as psychology, education, social work).
   - Learn a new skill that might add depth to your existing ministry (examples might include learning how to create a Web site or play a musical instrument).

Connecting with a Partner

1. Review your answers from Connecting with Yourself, exercise 1.
   - What insights did you gain into the current state of your ministry?
   - What excites you about learning, unlearning, and relearning?
   - What prevents you from learning, unlearning, and relearning?
   - What are some of the things you have already unlearned and relearned in your ministry?
2. Complete this sentence repeatedly until you run out of ideas: "If I taught at seminary, I'd be sure to teach them _____."
3. Tell about the most fascinating and insightful books you have read in the past year.

4.   Share ideas for creative learning opportunities and helpful existing educational events.

Connecting with God

Rediscover one of the spiritual resources that was helpful to you in the past and use it this week in your prayer time.

Pastor Jill always appreciated singing compline each night at seminary. She made arrangements with a seminary classmate to sing compline over the phone once a week. Father Jack reread a devotional book that had inspired him as a teenager.

Challenge

Take the steps necessary to make your continuing education program a reality in the coming year.

Creating a Lifelong Learning Plan

If you died today, what would you regret not having done? Twenty years ago Ted Leonsis, now a top media executive, was on a plane that had to make an emergency landing. That experience forced Ted to confront his own mortality. As a result, he made a list of 101 things he wanted to do in his life, including changing someone else's life through a charity. He has now accomplished many of the items on his list. He is the founder of cbuddies.org, a charity that creates e-mail friendships between people with and without mental retardation. This week you will get the opportunity to make your own list of things to do and learn before you die.

Connecting with Yourself

1. In your journal, number 1 to 100. Write down the 100 things you want to learn or do before you die. Do this as quickly as possible, without stopping to analyze your list. You may repeat items.
    - Review the list.
    - Mark a star next to the items you are able to do right now.
    - Mark with a highlighter the items that you most want to do.
2. Select up to 10 items from the list and create a plan for accomplishing them.
    - Make sure each goal on your list is within your control. You may want to become a famous author and have that as an ultimate goal. However, the response of other people to your work is not something you can control. A better goal might be to write a book this year or to talk to as many people as possible about the book you have published.

- Create a list of small, specific steps for accomplishing each item. Make sure that each step is specifically stated and within your control.
- Make a note of any resources necessary for each action.
- Set up a timeline. When will you take each step? What deadline will you set for finishing this task?
- Think about how you will handle setbacks, interruptions, and problems in accomplishing your goal.
- How will you celebrate your accomplishment when you have finished?

    Pastor Ed wanted to read a book a month for the next year. He selected 12 books. For each book, he created a schedule based on its length and the number of days that month. He factored into his plan the inevitable days in which reading would be impossible. Anya, a Christian education director, had always wanted to learn to swim. Her list of steps included buying a swimming suit, contacting local pools and athletic organizations for the price and availability of swimming lessons, clearing a space in her schedule for taking the lessons, finding the extra money in her budget for the class, signing up for a swim class, hiring a babysitter to care for her young children, and attending each lesson. Afterwards, she planned to take her family on a celebration weekend at a hotel with an indoor water park.

3. Choose a specific date to review your list of 100 items and create a plan for 10 more items on the list. Mark that date on your calendar.

Connecting with a Partner

Find or create a learning event that interests both of you and in which you can participate together. Ideas might include participating in a teleclass (classes offered by a telephone conference call and often advertised on the Internet), asking a local expert to teach you how to build or cook something, taking a class at an exercise facility, attending an author presentation at a local bookstore, joining a Bible study at another congregation, or reading and discussing a book together.

Connecting with God

Share your "learn and do list" with God. Thank God for giving you the desire and ability to do these activities. Ask for God's guidance as you seek to accomplish your goals.

Challenge

Do at least one of the activities on your "100 things to learn or do before you die" list.

Cultivating Delight

"Are we having fun yet?" Much of life, including self-care, is hard work. The title of this chapter comes from poet, essayist, and naturalist Diane Ackerman's book of the same name. In it she writes about how she changed her attitude toward caring for her garden, learning to approach it with the goal of "cultivating delight." This might be a helpful attitude for all of life. Instead of approaching each task with your head down, ready to plow into the work, you might choose to play at it, cultivating delight. Although you cannot control the external things that bring you joy, such as the kind words and loving gestures of others, you can control your approach to daily life. So relax, clear your mind, and take off your shoes if you want to—this week you are going to have fun.

Connecting with Yourself

1. Find a quiet spot and bring to mind each of the following experiences of joy or delight. Remember a time when you laughed uncontrollably, a delightful meal, a joyful place, a delightful moment with a friend or family member, a joyful worship event, a delightful sound, and any other moment that has brought you joy.
2. Make a collage of your favorite people and things. You can use photos, old magazines, and anything else you can find around your home.
3. What are specific ways you can make the tasks of daily ministry more delightful? List all of your ideas. Try one of them this week.
4. Create a play space in your home or office. This can be as small as a bucket of toys or as large as a room. Fill it with inexpensive tools for

play—modeling clay, scissors and paper, markers, sidewalk chalk, an Etch-a-Sketch™, a musical instrument, a small basketball hoop and ball, a handheld computer game, or anything else that delights you. Set aside some play time this week!

Connecting with a Partner

1. Show your collages to each other. Talk about the people, activities, and things that bring you delight.
2. Plan an outing for your partner that includes some of the joyful things on his or her collage. Keep the content of the outing a surprise. Make an agreement to limit the amount of money you will spend. Set a time for the outings within the next two weeks. Enjoy!

Connecting with God

Using your concordance, look up Bible passages that use the words delight, joy, and rejoice. Copy the ones you most appreciate into your journal. Use these verses as part of your daily prayers.

Challenge

In Paul's letter to the Philippians, he said this about his life, "I have learned to be content with whatever I have" (Phil. 4:11b). One way that you can create both mental and physical contentment is to meditate on something that brings you joy. Your body does not know the difference between real and imagined experiences. For that reason, imagining a joyful event can create the same physical benefits as the real experience. Spend at least five minutes each day this week recalling and meditating on something or someone that brings you joy.

Expressing Gratitude

Every time Pastor Kip visited Mrs. Olsen, she did something to say thank you. At first she would bake something special, a pie or a batch of cookies. When she became more frail, she would purchase cookies to give to him. Toward the end of her life, Mrs. Olsen could only slide a dollar into a card with her name scrawled inside. Still she always did something to show her thanks.

Expressing gratitude is a basic human need. We need to acknowledge those people who love and care for us. Yet amidst the frustrations and chaos of daily life, we sometimes neglect to thank both God and others. We may even brush off the thanks that others express to us. This week you will take time to be grateful and to recognize that expressing and receiving gratitude is an essential component of self-care.

Connecting with Yourself

1. Take a gratitude walk. Go to a park or other place where you feel comfortable walking alone. With each step you take, thank God for something in your life. Try to cover all the areas of your life including your history, your family, your friends, your work, your health, your possessions, and your talents. Only take steps when you can name something for which you are thankful. Between your prayers of gratitude, stop, rest, and reflect.

    When you come to the end of all that you have to say, turn around and retrace your steps, reflecting on the journey you have taken thus far in your life. If walking is difficult for you, you might bounce a ball, toss a small beanbag, or engage in some other rhythmic activity.

2. For what about you are people grateful? Ask your spouse, a trusted friend, or your partner to participate in this exercise with you. Make an agreement to share one thing about each other for which you are thankful each day this week. You can do this via e-mail, regular mail, or phone calls.
    *   How did hearing the ways that someone else is grateful for you change your day?
    *   How did expressing your thanks for someone else change your day?

Connecting with a Partner

1. Set a timer for five minutes. Complain about everything that bothers you about your life, both personally and professionally. When you have each had a turn, take a short break.

    Set the timer for five minutes. Talk about everything that you are thankful for in your life, both personally and professionally.
    *   How did you feel after each exercise?
    *   Which exercise gave you more energy?
    *   What personal insights did you gain from the two exercises?
    *   What was it like to listen to the complaints?
    *   What was it like to listen to the statements of gratitude?
2. What prevents you from being grateful? What can you do to develop a more grateful attitude?
3. How do you feel when someone expresses gratitude to you for something you have done in ministry? How do you respond?
4. Share some of the ways in which people have expressed gratitude to you for your ministry.

Connecting with God

First Timothy 2:1 says, "First of all, then, I urge that supplications, prayers, intercessions, and thanksgivings be made for everyone." This week in your prayers, make an effort to thank God for everyone you can think of. Concentrate upon those people for whom you may not always feel thankful.

Challenge

Take a day this week to say thank you to the people who help to sustain your life. As much as possible, say your thanks in person. If you like, you can include a small token of appreciation with your words of thanks (examples include flowers from your garden and homemade cookies). Start with the people closest to you, your family and friends. Do not neglect the strangers and acquaintances who care for you daily—the mail carrier, the newspaper deliverer, your child's teacher, the highway toll collector, your physician, and anyone else who functions in some way that serves you.

Take time to reflect on how this experience affects your life.

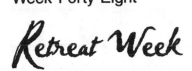

This retreat week provides another opportunity and a new setting from which to consider your spirit and body. Refer to the introduction for a description of the purpose and structure of a retreat week. As you create a retreat that is nurturing for you, you may want to use some of the following movies, books, and activities.

MOVIES AND VIDEO

Big
A twelve-year-old boy gets his wish to be "big" in this comedy.

Dead Poets Society
A teacher takes an unconventional approach to learning at a New England boarding school.

Educating Rita
A Cockney woman enrolls in a course at the Open University and becomes driven by her thirst for knowledge.

Good Will Hunting
A professor befriends a troubled mathematical genius who is working as a janitor at Massachusetts Institute of Technology.

Groundhog Day
A cynical television weatherman is forced to repeatedly relive Groundhog's Day in Punxsutawney, Pennsylvania.

Leap of Faith
A charlatan faith-healer and preacher lands in a small town and is confronted with a true miracle.

Mr. Holland's Opus
High school music teacher Mr. Holland comes to terms with his life's work.

Books

Fiction

Bee Season by Myla Goldberg
When Ellie wins a spelling bee, it leads to an adventure in which all of the members of her Jewish family explore their spirituality.

Davita's Harp by Chaim Potok
Davita, raised by political activists who have abandoned the faiths of their childhood, must find her own spiritual path—even in the midst of tragedy.

Does God Know How to Tie Shoes? by Nancy White Carlstrom
Words and messages about God come from wise parents in response to a child's questions in this picture book for young children.

The Mists of Avalon by Marion Zimmer Bradley
This is the tale of Sir Arthur and the knights of the round table, told from the women's point of view and centered around the battle between the old spirituality and the rise of Christianity.

The Old, Old Man and the Very Little Boy by Kristine Franklin
This picture book portrays an emotional relationship between a wise elder and a young boy in an African village.

The Red Tent by Anita Diamant
The life of the biblical character Dinah is given form and substance in this historical novel. Diamant, who frequently writes about modern Jewish life, provides a keen vision of how the women of Dinah's day lived.

Nonfiction

Another Shot: How I Relived My Life in Less Than a Year by Joe Kita
Kita chose 25 regrets and attempted to reverse them in a course of a year.

The Cup of Our Life: A Guide for Spiritual Growth by Joyce Rupp
Rupp's six-week guide offers creative paths for connecting to oneself and
to God.

Dancing in the Aisle: Spiritual Lessons We've Learned from Children
by Rochelle Melander and Harold Eppley
The authors reflect on how their encounters with children have taught them
about spirituality. Each essay is accompanied by a Bible reading, questions
for reflection, and a spiritual challenge.

Finding Joy: 101 Ways to Free Your Spirit and Dance with Life by
Charlotte Davis Kasl
Kasl, a psychologist, offers concrete exercises and activities for
cultivating joy.

Memories of God by Roberta Bondi
In her spiritual autobiography, this early church historian grapples with the
meaning of the incarnation in her own daily existence and, in the end,
understands more fully the joy of Christian life.

Plain and Simple: A Woman's Journey to the Amish by Sue Bender.
A woman lives with the Amish and discovers that spirituality can be
cultivated through ordinary chores.

Spiritual Literacy by Frederic and Mary Ann Brussat
Spiritual RX: Prescriptions for Living a Meaningful Life by Frederic
and Mary Ann Brussat
In both of these books, the Brussats offer resources and exercises for
deepening one's spirituality and developing a spiritual practice.

Working the Angles: The Shape of Pastoral Integrity by Eugene H.
Peterson
Peterson encourages spiritual leaders to make prayer, scripture, and spiritual
direction priorities in their ministry.

ACTIVITIES

This might be a good time to explore some of the challenges that you did not have time to complete during the previous seven weeks. You may also want to repeat a challenge that was particularly useful to you. Any of the weekly challenges are suited to a retreat.

- Make a retreat under the guidance of a spiritual director at a local retreat center, convent, or monastery.
- Play a trivia game.
- Learn to say a prayer in another language.
- Do a puzzle of some sort—crossword, picture, or physical.
- Watch the movie *Groundhog Day* and think about what it would be like to relive one of your days. What insights might you gain from the experience?
- Listen to different recordings of the same musical piece. Reflect on how one piece of music can be interpreted in unique ways.
- Make a homemade gift to express your gratitude to someone.
- Compose your own book of Proverbs, based on insights you have gained throughout your life and ministry.
- If you are a person who saves thank-you notes from the past, find them and read them again.
- Go to a park and play on the playground equipment.
- Play a game that used to delight you as a child.
- Read a book of your favorite comic strips or listen to a tape of your favorite comedian.
- Learn to cook or bake something delightful that you have never made before.
- Build a fort, using an old cardboard box or your dining room chairs and a blanket. Stock it with pillows, food, and books and make your retreat there. If you choose a box, you could paint or color on the inside walls.
- Purchase a bunch of Mylar balloons and spend an afternoon batting them around with friends.
- Purchase kazoos and, either alone or with others, make joyful music. Be as silly as you want to be.

Section Six

Sustaining a Life Vision

Week Forty-Nine

Leaving a Legacy

At a lecture given by children's book author and Newberry Award winner Madeleine L'Engle, she told us about the butterfly effect—a meteorological concept attributed to Edward Lorenz, which asserts that the flapping of a butterfly's wings in Brazil might result in tornados in Texas. She used this concept to convey the importance of personal choice. She believed that our choice to attend that lecture could change the course of world events. While that might sound dramatic, L'Engle's words remind us that our daily actions have consequences beyond what we can imagine. Even the small changes you have been making as you seek to take better care of yourself will impact both others and your environment. Your daily choices, when joined together, create a legacy that affects people and places beyond your immediate situation. This week you will consider what sort of legacy you wish to leave behind both today and after a lifetime.

Connecting with Yourself

1. Create a legacy box for your friends and family. This might be something that you would want them to have to remember you by after your death. Gather objects that represent your life thus far. You might include precious objects from your past—photographs, souvenirs, jewelry, family mementos, or clothing. You may also want to put objects into the box that symbolize something about yourself. An avid reader might place a favorite book into the box. A person known to be slow and plodding might include a toy turtle. Finally, include letters or notes of instruction and explanation to those who will open the box.

2. Imagine that you will die in a week. What would you want to say to the people you care about most? Write a letter to each of these people. You may want to set it aside to be opened by them in the event of your death. You may also choose to give it to them now.
3. Write an epitaph by which you would want to be remembered. You might want to consult epitaph books for guidance (see appendix).

Connecting with Your Partner

1. Show your legacy box to your partner. Explain why each item is a part of the box.
2. Imagine that when you leave your current position, they hang a photograph of you on the wall. In the future, what do you imagine that people will be saying about you when they see your photo?
3. How do you understand the concept of legacy in your religious tradition? In what ways has that understanding shaped the way you live your life?

Connecting with God

During your prayer time this week, look for hymns and scripture lessons that you might want to include as part of your funeral or memorial service. At the end of the week, make a choice and give copies to trusted family members and friends.

Challenge

What is your daily legacy? At the end of each day this week, make a list of the ways that you contributed to the welfare of the world or affected change in the world. Examples could include anything from speaking kind words to strangers to being a courteous driver. Reflect on these questions:
   • How did your actions today reflect your lifelong legacy?
   • What might you want to do differently tomorrow?

Creating a Vision Statement

A friend of ours asked, "How many people did God call to lead the Israelites out of slavery in Egypt? How many people did God trust with communicating the Ten Commandments? Just one: Moses. Does that tell you something?" Our friend was encouraging us to remember that God has called each of us to a unique life.

In the book of Jeremiah, we read that God had plans for Jeremiah before he was conceived: "Before I formed you in the womb I knew you, and before you were born I consecrated you; I appointed you a prophet to the nations" (Jer. 1:5). God might have a plan for each of us long before we are born, but for most of us it takes some time to discern that plan. Some people spend years struggling to discover what God is calling them to do with their lives. Discerning God's will for your life has been part of your task as you have sought to take better care of yourself this year. This week you will review some of the work you did in creating a life vision during section one and compose a vision statement to help sustain your vision.

Connecting with Yourself

1.   Write your obituary. Assume that you will live to be at least 80 years old when you die. Make the obituary a longer, more elaborate treatment than the ordinary newspaper notice. When you have finished, reflect on the following questions in your journal.
   - What does your obituary tell you about your life's vision?
   - How close are you to achieving that vision?
   - What steps would you need to take to get there?

2. A vision statement is a short phrase or sentence that illustrates your approach to life. It does not describe your entire life's vision. It reflects the heart of your vision and helps you to stay on task in moving toward it. Keep in mind that you can modify your vision statement (and your vision) as necessary. Using your obituary as a guide, write a vision statement for your life. You may also want to review the vision of your ideal life that you created during week five and the list of priorities you compiled during week eight.

    As you write your statement, work on creating something that is short enough to remember. Suzanne, a parish administrator, wrote, "With the gifts God gives, I will create beauty." Father Leonard, a seminary professor, wrote, "Recognizing each moment as a gift from God, I will seek to be present in what I am doing." Sister Marsha, a parish nurse, wrote, "Each day I will love God, love others, and learn something new."

3. Create an artistic portrayal of your vision statement that you can post in your office and home.

4. Make a commitment to review your vision statement at least once a month to see if it accurately reflects the life you want to live.

Connecting with a Partner

1. Share your vision statement. How has your vision statement been shaped by the work you have done on self-care during the past year? How will you remind yourself of your vision statement on a daily basis?

2. How do you hope your vision statement will affect the way you function as a spiritual leader?

Connecting with God

During your prayer time this week, go to a place that you find visually inspiring. You may choose more than one place. If you cannot go somewhere, use photos from your own collection, a book, a magazine, or the Internet.

Challenge

At the end of each day, name specific, concrete ways in which your vision statement has made a difference in your life today. If you have difficulty with this exercise, consider changing your vision statement—or your life.

Continuing in a Lifetime of Self-Care

The most difficult part about changing your life is not making the changes but maintaining them. You might resolve to eat better and do so for a day, a week, or even a month. Then life gets complicated again, you get busy or stressed, and suddenly you find yourself wolfing down double cheeseburgers and chocolate shakes at your local fast-food restaurant five times a week.

Perhaps you have worked through all the exercises in this book and you still can't find anything in your closet. Maybe you're still saying yes to too many things you would rather not do, making it impossible to focus on the essential matters of your work. And to top it off, you never did make that dental appointment to have your teeth cleaned.

With the apostle Paul you might feel like saying, "I do not understand my own actions. For I do not do what I want, but I do the very thing I hate" (Rom. 7:15). Give yourself a break. Nobody's perfect. Still you need not give up. Try, try again! Self-care is a lifelong discipline, wrought with setbacks and disappointments as well as accomplishments. This week you review your progress thus far and set goals for making both major and minor changes in your life.

Connecting with Yourself

1. In your journal, list all of the positive self-care changes you have made in the past year by completing the following sentence as many times as necessary: I am proud of myself for _____.
2. There is no magic formula for a lifetime of self-care. It is primarily a matter of recognizing your needs, identifying the steps you need to take, setting a time frame, finding support, and getting to it.

Make a list of major changes in your life that you still need to make to take care of yourself. Write each one of these changes on a separate sheet of paper and create three columns. In the first column, make a list of the steps you will need to take to make the change happen. In the middle column, write the date by which you would like to take each step. In the third column, list the people or tools that will help you through each step of the process.

Pastor Howard realized that he was unable to remain healthy in his current parish. The abundance of meetings and emergencies, the ongoing conflict among the leadership, and the church's building program created too much stress in his life and prevented him from having undistracted time with his wife and children. Pastor Howard decided he needed a new post. He made his list of steps, including updating his resume and seeking counseling to discover what type of a parish call would best suit him. For these steps he set a combined time limit of two months. He enlisted the help of a colleague in updating his resume. In order to discern what type of a call he would want next, he gathered friends, family, and colleagues to sit with him for an evening and ask him questions.

3. Make a list of minor changes in your life that you still need to make to take care of yourself. Examples of minor changes might include creating a more healthy diet, organizing a closet, shifting your schedule to provide exercise time, or creating a plan to keep committee meetings to an allotted length of time. Write each one of these changes on a separate sheet of paper and create three columns. In the first column, make a list of the steps you will need to take to make the change happen. In the middle column, record the date by which you would like to take each step. In the third column, list the people or tools that will help you through each step of the process.

4. List at least five things that you plan to do to take care of yourself each day. You might want to use colorful markers or your desktop publishing program to make the list appealing to look at. Post the list in a place that you can see it and attend to it each day. Review this list every month to evaluate its relevance for your life. Feel free to revise it at any time.

Connecting with Your Partner

1. What has been most helpful to you in the process of working together to change your lives?
2. What growth have you observed in your partner in the past year?
3. What sort of relationship would you like to maintain?
4. What are some ways you can support each other on an ongoing basis?

Connecting with God

Hopefully over the course of working with this book you have made many changes in your life. Some of them have become permanent habits. Other changes you may have abandoned along the way. During your prayer time this week, forgive yourself for any ways that you believe you have failed to take care of yourself. Consider what you have learned from your mistakes and failures. Ask God for the resolve and support to take on the self-care changes you still need to make.

Challenge

Choose one area of your life in which you need support to take care of your self. Find a partner with the same need. Set up a plan to support each other in making this one change. Elaine, a parish administrator, wanted to begin a daily meditation time each day. She and a friend arranged to e-mail each other at 7 A.M. before they began their meditation time and again at 7:30 A.M. after they had completed it. Father Myron wanted to eat more healthfully. He enlisted the help of a fellow priest. They spent one day together each month creating menus, shopping, and cooking a month's worth of healthy meals. Pastor Charlotte planned to retire within five years. She organized a preretirement clergy group that met monthly to discuss concerns related to retirement.

Week Fifty-Two

Retreat Week

This retreat week provides another opportunity and a new setting from which to consider how to sustain your life vision. Refer to the introduction for a description of the purpose and structure of a retreat week. As you create a retreat that is nurturing for you, you may want to use some of the following movies, books, and activities.

MOVIES

Being There
Chance, a gardener who moves through life with his own sense of rhythm, is constantly misunderstood by those around him. The movie is based on the book by Jerzy Kosinski.

Da
A man returns to Ireland for his estranged father's funeral and, in the process, comes to terms with their relationship.

Field of Dreams
One man follows his vision to create a baseball field in the middle of a cornfield, despite criticism and other obstacles and confirms the adage "if you build it they will come." The movie is based on the book *Shoeless Joe* by W. P. Kinsella.

Pay It Forward
In response to a class assignment to change the world, twelve-year-old Trevor does three big favors for strangers and asks them to "pay it forward." The movie is based on the book *Pay It Forward* by Catherine Ryan Hyde.

Saving Private Ryan
A company of men risk their lives in order to save Private Ryan. In return, they ask only that he live his life in such a way that their sacrifice is made worthwhile.

State and Main
An aspiring screenwriter learns about second chances while working on a movie set in a small town in Vermont.

Books

Fiction

A Prayer for Owen Meany by John Irving
Owen Meany has an absolutely clear vision for his life. Johnny, the novel's narrator, tells the story of that vision and the events that unfold from it. He attributes his belief in Christ to Meany's presence in his life.

Godric by Frederick Buechner
This is a fictional account of Godric of Finchale, a holy man from the twelfth century and how he changes the world.

Holes by Louis Sachar
Stanley Yelnats ends up at a juvenile detention center as a result of a miscarriage of justice and, while there, discovers his destiny.

Oh, the Places You'll Go! by Dr. Seuss
This is a whimsical picture book about life's many possibilities.

Pink and Say by Patricia Polacco
A former slave teaches a white teenager how to read during the Civil War.

The Treasure by Uri Shulevitz
This picture book reminds readers that sometimes one must travel far to find the treasure that is near.

Nonfiction

I Know Why the Caged Bird Sings by Maya Angelou
In this first book in Angelou's series of books about her life, she describes how she overcame obstacles to begin seeking her dream.

O Come Ye Back to Ireland: Our First Year in County Clare by Niall Williams and Christine Breen
A young American couple travels from New York to a farm in the west of Ireland to start a new life.

Personal History by Katharine Graham
Graham overcame many obstacles, including her husband's suicide, to succeed in life. After her husband's death, Graham went on to become the publisher of the *Washington Post.*

Remembrances and Celebrations: A Book of Eulogies, Elegies, Letters, and Epitaphs by Jill Werman Harris, editor
This collection of remembrances provides touching examples of this genre from the pens of many famous persons.

Soul Survivor: How My Faith Survived the Church by Philip Yancey
Yancey profiles 13 individuals who have helped him to maintain his faith in God even when the church has abused and disappointed him.

Tying Rocks to Clouds: Meetings and Conversations with Wise and Spiritual People by William Elliott.
This is a book of interviews with famous spiritual leaders from several faith traditions.

ACTIVITIES

This might be a good time to explore some of the challenges that you did not have time to complete during the previous three weeks. You may also want to repeat a challenge that was particularly useful to you. The challenges from week forty-nine and fifty-one are suited to a retreat.

- Read the memoir of someone you respect.
- Envision yourself doing what you hope to do in your life's vision statement. As you do this, picture all those who support you—even those who have now died—surrounding you. They smile and applaud. They are encouraging you. Imagine yourself successfully completing the task.
- Choose your favorite self-care activity and create a retreat around it.
- Use the Internet to review the vision statements of companies and individuals.
- Go to a mountaintop or the top floor of a building, somewhere high enough to get a good view. How does this perspective change the way you see the world?
- If your life could be recorded on a map, what would it look like? Make a map of your life.
- If your life could be performed as a dance, what would it look like? What music would represent the various phases of your life? Select music for each stage of your life, including the next one. Then, perform for yourself a dance that illustrates your life.
- Get a camera and a roll of film and wander around taking pictures that reflect your vision for your life. When they are developed, arrange them on poster board or in a frame as a reminder.
- Take a day to practice "random acts of kindness," leaving a legacy of kindness behind you all day. Anonymously pay for a stranger's coffee, put money in parking meters, pick up garbage on your street, or offer to baby-sit for a friend.
- Read the Gospel of Mark with a sense of Jesus' vision for his life and ministry.
- Find a retreat center where you can run an obstacle course. Do so as a way of reminding yourself that you can overcome obstacles. If you cannot find a center, enlist the help of a local YMCA or other athletic center.
- Take time to consider what type of a legacy you would like to leave behind in the community where you now serve as a spiritual leader. How will you accomplish this?
- Write your eulogy from several perspectives, such as that of your spouse, children, colleagues, teachers, and others.

Appendix

Annotated Resources

Blessings

Anders, Isabel. *Simple Blessings for Sacred Moments*. Liguori, Mo.: Liguori/Triumph, 1998. Anders has collected these blessings to be used for daily living, transitional moments, and seasonal celebrations.

Frank, Ann Wall. *Bless This House*. Lincolnwood, Ill.: NTC Contemporary Publishing House, 1996. This book offers home-dwellers (be it in an apartment, house, or houseboat) a ritual for blessing their dwellings.

Skinner, Susan. *Blessings for Today*. Nashville, Tenn.: Dimensions for Living, 2001. Skinner has collected graces and blessings for life's many occasions, both large and small.

Coaching

www.christiancoaching.com. Offers a database for persons interested in finding a Christian coach.

www.coachfederation.org. This Web site is the organization responsible for credentialing coaches, and offers a database of coaches.

www.coachu.com. One of the primary organizations that trains coaches, this Web site offers information on free seminars as well as a free coach referral service.

Leonard, Thomas J. *The Portable Coach: 28 Surefire Strategies for Business and Personal Success*. New York: Scribner, 1998. Leonard (www.thomasleonard.com), founder of Coach University (www.coachuniversity.com), presents his strategies for success. The book includes helpful checklists and self-tests.

Committees

Hestenes, Roberta. *Turning Committees into Communities*. Colorado Springs: NavPress, 1991. This slim volume provides helpful information on how to recruit volunteers for committees.

Melander, Rochelle, and Harold Eppley. *Growing Together: Spiritual Exercises for Church Committees*. Minneapolis: Augsburg Fortress, 1998. Offers a simple small group process that you can apply to any committee, task force, or group meeting. Each of the 50 thematic exercises contains a prayer, community building time, Bible reading, and questions for reflection.

Olsen, Charles M. *Transforming Church Boards into Communities of Spiritual Leaders*. Bethesda, Md.: The Alban Institute, 1995. Olsen provides practical and inspiring suggestions for helping church boards deepen their faith and develop their leadership abilities.

Community

Bonhoeffer, Dietrich. *Life Together*. San Francisco: HarperSanFrancisco, 1979. Bonhoeffer's classic exploration of Christian community provides a lasting vision of how Christians can live together.

Burns, Olive Ann. *Cold Sassy Tree*. New York: Dell, 1986. Fourteen-year-old Willy Tweedy tells the story of his grandfather's hasty remarriage to a younger woman in this novel set in a Georgia community where nothing's a secret for long.

Fleischman, Paul. *Seedfolk*. New York: HarperCollins, 1999. An inner-city community builds a garden and new relationships in this young adult novel.

Giardina, Denise. *Storming Heaven*. New York: Fawcett Books, 1987. Four people tell about their battle to unionize the coal companies around 1900.

Hassler, Jon. *The Dean's List*. New York: Ballantine Books, 1997.

———. *Rookery Blues*. New York: Ballantine Books, 1995. In these two novels, Hassler follows a group of professors through their professional and personal lives at an isolated fictitious state college in Minnesota.

Knight, Mary Burns. *Welcoming Babies*. Gardiner, Maine: Tilbury House Publishers, 1994. This picture book illustrates the ways various cultures and faith traditions welcome babies, and includes helpful notes for parents.

Landvik, Lorna. *The Tall Pine Polka*. New York: Ballantine, 2001. A small, tight-knit northern Minnesota community is turned upside down when a Hollywood movie company decides to film on location, using one of the locals as the star.

Letts, Billie. *Where the Heart Is*. New York: Warner Books, 1995. A young woman, pregnant and homeless, lives in a small-town Wal-Mart store until locals step in to care for her.

Mirvis, Tova. *The Ladies Auxiliary*. New York: Ballantine Books, 1999. A tight-knit community of orthodox Jews is challenged by the arrival of a new and more free-spirited member to their community.

Conflict

Day, Katie. *Difficult Conversations: Taking Risks, Acting with Integrity*. Bethesda, Md.: The Alban Institute, 2001. Day presents the reasons conversations become difficult and describes models for true dialogue.

Haugk, Kenneth C. *Antagonists in the Church: How to Identify and Deal with Destructive Conflict*. Minneapolis: Augsburg Publishing House, 1988. In this practical book, Haugk teaches about healthy and unhealthy conflict and provides solutions for coping with antagonism.

Counseling for Spiritual Leaders

www.christosministries.org. This counseling service for clergy and their families offers a toll free help line: (888) 879-3000.

www.ministrydevelopment.org. This Web site is the home of a national network of accredited centers providing resources for clergy and other church workers, denominational leadership, and local churches. The centers are located in a variety of cities in the United States and many have their own Web sites linked to this site.

Depression

Burns, David D. *Feeling Good: The New Mood Therapy*. New York: Avon Books, 1980. Burns explains how those living with depression can find help by revising their thought processes.

Gregg-Schroeder, Susan. *In the Shadow of God's Wings: Grace in the Midst of Depression*. Nashville: Upper Room Books, 1997. A United Methodist pastor shares her own journey through clinical depression and in the process provides insights about community and spirituality.

Devotional Books

Brussat, Frederic, and Mary Ann Brussat. *Spiritual Literacy: Reading the Sacred in Everyday Life*. New York: Scribner, 1996. The Brussats have collected quotes from a variety of religious traditions under an alphabet of themes. The book includes spiritual exercises, rituals, journal questions, and activities.

Jones, Alan W. *Passion for Pilgrimage: Notes for the Journey Home.* Harrisburg, Pa.: Morehouse Publishing, 1999. Jones ponders the Christian's search for God as he considers the Passion and Easter stories.

L'Engle, Madeleine, and Carol F. Chase, ed. *Glimpses of Grace: Daily Thoughts and Reflections.* San Francisco: HarperSanFrancisco, 1996. L'Engle writes fiction for young adults and spiritual essays for adults. This book collects excerpts of her writings for the devotional reader to use each day.

Melander, Rochelle, and Harold Eppley. *Timeouts with God: Meditations for Parents.* St. Louis: Concordia Publishing House, 2001. This collection of 101 devotions is aimed at busy, harried parents who need to hear God's words of enduring grace.

Mild, Mary L., ed. *Women at the Well: Meditations on Healing and Wholeness.* Valley Forge, Pa.: Judson Press, 1996. This book contains a year of meditations written by women and centered around the themes of health, healing, and wholeness.

Peterson, Eugene H. *Praying with Jesus: A Year of Daily Prayers and Reflections on the Words and Actions of Jesus.* San Francisco: HarperSanFrancisco, 1993. Daily readings and prayers help readers to deepen their relationship with Jesus.

Richardson, Jan L. In *Wisdom's Path: Discovering the Sacred in Every Season.* Cleveland: The Pilgrim Press, 2000. Richardson uses essays, poetry, and cut-paper artwork to explore the liturgical seasons and themes of community and inclusivity.

————. *Night Visions: Searching the Shadows of Advent and Christmas.* Cleveland: United Church Press, 1998. Essays, prayers, and original artwork lead the reader to a deeper reflection upon the meaning of this holiday season.

————. *Sacred Journeys: A Woman's Book of Daily Prayer.* Nashville: Upper Room Books, 1995. A year of meditations and prayers focus on the writings of women theologians and spiritual leaders.

Rupp, Joyce. *The Cup of Our Lives.* Notre Dame, Ind.: Ave Maria Press, 1998. This six-week course guides the reader through meditations centered around a cup and the metaphor of our lives as a cup.

Dreams

Barasch, Mark Ian. *Healing Dreams: Exploring the Dreams that Can Transform Your Life*. New York: Berkley, 2001. This book is designed to help the reader tap into the power of dreams for deepening one's spiritual paths and improving one's career, relationships, and health.

Bulkeley, Kelly. *Transforming Dreams: Learning Spiritual Lessons from the Dreams You Never Forget*. New York: John Wiley & Sons, 2000. Bulkeley tells how dreams have transformed lives and then shows how readers can attend to their dreams and notice the "big ones."

Garfield, Patricia. *The Universal Dream Key: The Twelve Most Common Dream Themes around the World*. New York: Cliff Street Books, 2001. Garfield provides a guide for dreamers to discover what their dreams reveal about their daily life.

Emotional Health

www.MentalHealth.com. This site, maintained by a partnership between Japan and Canada, provides an encyclopedia of mental health information. As well as describing a large number of diagnoses, the site provides links to additional Web sites that deal with specific mental health issues such as anxiety.

Moore, Thomas. *Care of the Soul: A Guide for Cultivating Depth and Sacredness in Everyday Life*. New York: HarperPerennial, 1992. Moore explores the concept of the soul and how it informs our emotional and spiritual life.

Muller, Wayne. *Legacy of the Heart: The Spiritual Advantages of a Painful Childhood*. New York: A Fireside Book, 1992. Through essays and exercises, Muller confronts many of the spiritual and emotional issues faced by adults who are recovering from a painful childhood.

Peck, M. Scott. *The Road Less Traveled: A New Psychology of Love, Traditional Values and Spiritual Growth*. New York: Simon and Schuster, 1978. The author believes that confronting and solving life's problems can lead humans to spiritual and emotional growth.

Exercise and Fitness

www.choosetomove.com. This site presents the fitness program sponsored by the American Heart Association (www.americanheart.org).

www.niddk.nih.gov/health/nutrit/walking/walkingbro/walking.htm. This is an online walking brochure on getting started with a walking program. It includes safety tips, warm-up exercises, and a sample program.

www.sitandbefit.com. This Web site compliments the popular PBS series *Sit and Be Fit*, which provides a slow and gentle exercise program for adults, children, and those with special needs such as arthritis or COPD. The Web site sells videos of the program.

Austin, Miriam. *Yoga for Wimps: Poses for the Flexibly Impaired*. New York: Sterling Publishing, 2000. This is a great book for those who are beginning students of yoga or for individuals interested in using some of the poses for gentle stretching and increasing flexibility.

Blair, Steven, Bess Marcus, Ruth Ann Carpenter, Peter Jaret, and Andrea Dunn. *Active Living Every Day: 20 Weeks to Lifelong Vitality*. Champaign, Ill.: Human Kinetics, 2001. This book includes a twenty-week plan to help readers become more physically active in the ways they choose through a variety of exercises and everyday activities, including dancing and vacuuming. The emphasis is on long-term lifestyle changes.

Gordon, Neil. *Arthritis: Your Complete Exercise Guide*. Champaign, Ill.: Human Kinetics, 1993. A safe exercise program for persons who have arthritis.

————. *Diabetes: Your Complete Exercise Guide*. Champaign, Ill.: Human Kinetics, 1993. This book provides a safe and sensible exercise program for people with diabetes.

Nelson, Miriam, Sarah Wernick, and Wendy Wray. *Strong Women Stay Young*, rev. ed. New York: Bantam Books, 2000. This is a great resource for women concerned about osteoporosis. It includes helpful diagrams for weight lifting. The Web site connected to the book, www.strongwomen.com, provides dietary information, recipes, articles, sample exercises, and further information on the books in this series.

Family Systems

Ansay, A. Manette. *Vinegar Hill*. New York: Avon Books, 1994. In this multi-layered novel, a young woman struggles to negotiate her husband's family of origin when they move in with his parents.

Friedman, Edwin H. *Generation to Generation: Family Process in Church and Synagogue*. New York: The Guilford Press, 1985. This book provides a detailed explanation of family systems theory and then applies it both to families in the congregation and to congregations as family systems.

————. *Friedman's Fables*. New York: The Guilford Press, 1990. Friedman's parables illustrate the various facets of family systems theory.

Gilbert, Roberta M. *Extraordinary Relationships: A New Way of Thinking about Human Interactions*. Minneapolis: Chronimed Publishing, 1992. An easy-to-read primer of family systems theory aimed at readers who wish to apply it to their own lives.

McGoldrick, Monica, and Randy Gerson. *Genograms in Family Assessment*. New York: W. W. Norton and Company, 1985. A resource geared to help the reader gather information for a genogram and assess it based on family systems theory.

Richardson, Ronald W. *Creating a Healthier Church: Family Systems Theory, Leadership, and the Congregational Life*. Minneapolis: Fortress Press, 1996. This book explains how family systems theory relates to congregations.

————. *Family Ties That Bind: A Self-Help Guide to Change through Family of Origin Therapy*. North Vancouver: Self-Counsel Press, 1984. Richardson guides readers through exercises about their family of origin.

Steinke, Peter L. *Healthy Congregations: A Systems Approach*. Bethesda, Md.: The Alban Institute, 1996. This book explains how a congregation can become healthier using a family systems approach.

————. *How Your Church Family Works: Understanding Congregations as Emotional Systems*. Bethesda, Md.: The Alban Institute, 1993. Steinke explains how family systems theory can be used in congregations.

Feelings

Boynton, Sandra. *A Is for Angry: An Animal and Adjective Alphabet*. New York: Workman Publishing, 1983. A popular children's book author uses her beloved characters and the alphabet to show feeling words to children.

Emberley, Ed, and Anne Miranda. *Glad Monster, Sad Monster: A Book about Feelings*. Boston: Little, Brown, and Co., 1997. Monsters express the activities that reflect various feelings. Monster masks and interactive questions are included.

Freymann, Saxton, and Joost Elffers. *How Are You Peeling? Foods with Moods*. New York: Arthur A. Levine Books, 1999. Hilarious photographs of anthropomorphized fruits and vegetables and a rhyming text combine to teach children about feelings.

Landvik, Lorna. *Welcome to the Great Mysterious*. New York: Ballantine Books, 2000. An actress takes time off to care for her nephew. In the process, she connects to her feelings and discovers new truths about love and family.

Lowry, Lois. *The Giver*. New York: Laurel Leaf Publishing, 1993. In a future society, a young boy must consider the importance of feelings and memories in relationships.

Finances

Hotchkiss, Dan. *Ministry and Money: A Guide for Clergy and Their Friends*. Bethesda, Md.: The Alban Institute, 2002. Hotchkiss explores the issues spiritual leaders have with money and helps them to "clean up" their own financial life so that they can lead by example.

Orman, Suze. *The Courage to Be Rich*. New York: Penguin Putnam, 1999. Orman's book helps the reader to identify and overcome obstacles of financial fear, anger, and shame to reach an attitude of abundance.

————. *The Road to Wealth: A Comprehensive Guide to Your Money*. New York: Putnam, 2001. This practical guide to money covers all of life's financial stages and provides key information for readers interested in the "how-to" of money management.

Food

www.allrecipes.com. Much like a virtual cookbook, this site also offers a free personalized recipe box service and a special section of diabetic recipes.

www.dianaskitchen.com. This Web site offers a wide range of recipes, including recipes for Crock-Pots.

www.eatright.org. The Web site for the American Dietetic Association.

www.globalgourmet.com. This Web site features columns on a variety of topics and message boards for conversations about food.

www.my-meals.com. This site allows the browser to review recipes based on courses, cuisines, or special diets.

www.nutritiouslygourmet.com. This educational Web site offers a monthly menu and food pyramids from other parts of the world.

www.usda.gov. The Web site for the United States Dietary Association.

Duyff, Roberta Larson. *The American Dietetic Association's Complete Food and Nutrition Guide*. New York: John Wiley & Sons, 1998. This ADA guide provides information on a wide variety of dietary questions, from feeding children to appropriate body composition.

Esquivel, Laura. *Like Water for Chocolate*. New York: Doubleday, 1992. The romantic tale of Tita, a gifted cook, who has fallen madly in love but who, because of tradition, must step aside so her older sister might marry her love.

Seton, Nora. *The Kitchen Congregation: A Daughter's Story of Wives and Women Friends*. New York: Picador USA, 2000. Seton recalls the stories and the people populating her mother's kitchen.

Whitcomb, Holly. *Feasting with God: Adventures in Table Spirituality*. Cleveland: United Church Press, 1996. This book offers recipes and discussion questions for a variety of family and community feasts.

Friendship

Fox, Mem. *Wilfred Gordon McDonald Partridge*. Brooklyn: Kane/Miller Book Publishers, 1985. In this children's picture book, a small child helps an old woman rediscover her memory.

L'Engle, Madeleine and Luci Shaw. *Friends for the Journey*. Ann Arbor, Mich.: Servant Publications, 1997. L'Engle, a Newbery Award winning author, and Shaw, a poet, discuss their friendship through dialogues and essays.

———. *A Prayerbook for Spiritual Friends*. Minneapolis: Augsburg Fortress, 1999. A collection of prayers by the two authors, who are longtime friends, demonstrates the purpose and benefits of having a spiritual prayer partner.

Lobel, Arnold. *Days with Frog and Toad*. New York: HarperCollins Children's Books, 1984.

———. *Frog and Toad All Year*. New York: HarperCollins Children's Books, 1984.

———. *Frog and Toad Are Friends*. New York: HarperCollins Children's Books, 1979.

———. *Frog and Toad Together*. New York: HarperCollins Children's Books, 1979. Lobel's quartet of books for early readers are filled with deeply inspiring tales of the friendship of Frog and Toad and how it is woven into their ordinary daily lives.

Tsukiyama, Gail. *The Language of the Threads*. New York: St. Martin's Griffin, 1999.

———. *Women of the Silk*. New York: St. Martin's Press, 1991. A young woman, forced to leave her family and work in the silk factory in China, finds friendship and community in her new home.

Gifts

L'Engle, Madeleine. *A Wrinkle in Time*. New York: Dell, 1962. In this children's novel, Meg, Calvin, and Charles set out on an adventure to rescue Meg and Charles's father. In the process, Meg learns that she has all that she needs within herself.

Potok, Chaim. *The Gift of Asher Lev*. New York: Alfred A. Knopf, 1990.

————. *My Name Is Asher Lev*. New York: Alfred A. Knopf, 1972. Asher Lev faces challenges from his family and community in order to pursue his God-given gift of painting.

Salzman, Mark. *Lying Awake*. New York: Alfred A. Knopf, 2000. A cloistered nun, gifted by inspiring visions and the ability to write, discovers that her creative gift is due to a brain tumor, and she must decide her fate.

Gratitude

Ryan, M. J. *Attitudes of Gratitude: How to Give and Receive Joy Every Day*. Berkeley, Calif.: Conari Press, 1999. The short essays in this book encourage readers to make gratitude part of their daily lives.

Zemach, Margot. *It Could Always Be Worse*. New York: Farrar, Straus, and Giroux, 1976. In this picture book, a poor man learns about gratitude—with a little help from his Rabbi.

Grief

Levy, Naomi. *To Begin Again: The Journey toward Comfort, Strength, and Faith in Difficult Times*. New York: Alfred A. Knopf, 1998. Rabbi Levy weaves the story of her own personal tragedy, the murder of her father, with the stories of her parishioners and the men and women of the Bible.

Lewis, C. S. *A Grief Observed*. New York: Bantam Doubleday Dell, 1976. Lewis's memoir explores his feelings and his faith following the death of his beloved wife from cancer.

Rylant, Cynthia. *Missing May*. New York: Dell, 1993. Summer is 12 years old when her beloved Aunt May dies, and she must come to terms with this devastating loss.

Wangerin, Walter. *Mourning into Dancing*. Grand Rapids: Zondervan, 1992. Wangerin explores a variety of life's losses, illustrated by poignant stories from his life and ministry.

Westburg, Granger E. *Good Grief: A Constructive Approach to the Problem of Loss.* Minneapolis: Fortress Press, 1983. This short book is a classic work on grief and healing.

Health and Healing

www.americanheart.org. This site provides health information related to exercise, weight loss, heart disease, and stroke from the American Heart Association.

www.cbshealthwatch.com. This site provides helpful information for managing one's individual health needs. Visitors can browse the site's Health Topics or Drug Directory or access some of the same information that doctors have.

www.healthfinder.gov. This is a free guide to reliable health information such as select online publications, clearinghouses, Web sites, support, and self-help groups, as well as government agencies and nonprofit organizations.

www.mayohealth.org. The Mayo Clinic Health Oasis, run by the Mayo Clinic in Rochester, Minnesota, provides reliable information on medical issues. The site is updated daily and allows the user to search the site or visit various centers such as those for arthritis or nutrition.

www.medlineplus.gov. This Web site is run by the National Library of Medicine at the National Institutes of Health and provides accurate, current medical information.

American Heart Association. *Your Heart: An Owner's Manual.* New York: Simon & Shuster, 1996. This book helps the reader to evaluate risk factors, recognize symptoms, create a healthy diet, and manage emotions.

Ansay, A. Manette. *Limbo.* New York: William Morrow, 2001. Ansay, a novelist, documents her faith struggles in the midst of fighting a mysterious illness that ended her piano career in her early twenties.

Dixon, Barbara M. *Good Health for African Americans.* New York: Crown Trade Paperback, 1994. Dixon presents a 24-week program for both nutrition and lifestyle transition for African Americans.

Flecher, Anne. *Thin for Life: 10 Keys to Success for People Who Have Lost Weight and Kept It Off.* New York: Houghton Mifflin, 1995. The author surveyed 160 people who had lost at least 20 pounds and kept it off for at least three years. She includes their success stories and the 10 keys to their success.

King, Stephen. *The Green Mile*. New York: Pocket Books, 1999. A death-row prisoner demonstrates an extraordinary capacity for healing.

Northrup, Christiane. *Women's Bodies, Women's Wisdom: Creating Physical and Emotional Health and Healing*. New York: Bantam Books, 1998. Northrup presents helpful information for women who wish to be more healthy, including instructions on how to develop a personal health plan.

Remen, Rachel Naomi. *Kitchen Table Wisdom: Stories That Heal*. New York: Riverhead Books, 1996. Remen, a physician who counsels the dying, reminds us through her stories that the act of sharing our wisdom can bring healing.

Reynolds, Sheri. *A Gracious Plenty*. New York: Harmony Books, 1997. Finch Nobles, badly burned as a child and now living alone, moves easily between the world of the dead and the world of the living.

Weil, Andrew. *Eight Weeks to Optimum Health*. New York: Alfred A. Knopf, 1997. Weil has developed a step-by-step program for improving one's health. The book includes recipes, specialized plans, and resources for information and supplies.

Homes

Mendelson, Cheryl. *Home Comforts: The Art and Science of Keeping House*. New York: Scribner, 1999. A guide to homemaking which offers meticulous instructions on everything from safely storing food to caring for clothing.

Spier, Peter. *Oh, Were They Ever Happy*. New York: Doubleday, 1978. In this children's picture book, three children decide to paint the house while their parents are out for the day. The hilarious illustrations convey the passion that goes into the project as well as the parents' reaction to the paint job.

Susanka, Sarah. *The Not So Big House*. Newtown: The Taunton Press, 1998. This book contains photos, floor plans, and text illustrating the movement toward "not so big" homes that use space more efficiently.

Identity

Berg, Elizabeth. *The Pull of the Moon*. New York: Jove Books, 1996. A woman journeys to new venues and in the process learns to appreciate what she has at home.

Carle, Eric. *The Mixed-Up Chameleon*. New York: HarperTrophy, 1975. In this children's picture book, the discontent chameleon wishes to be like many of the animals in the zoo.

Henkes, Kevin. *Chrysanthemum*. New York: Greenwillow, 1991. Chrysanthemum learns to treasure her unusual name in this book which both children and adults will enjoy.

Howatch, Susan. *Glittering Images*. New York: Fawcett Crest, 1996. Anglican priest Charles Ashworth confronts himself and his own doubts in this fast-paced novel set in the church of England. This is the first book in the author's Starbridge series.

King, Thomas. *Green Grass, Running Water*. New York: Bantam Books, 1994. In this comedic novel, modern Canadian Indians struggle in their search for identity in a white community.

Lamb, Wally. *I Know This Much Is True*. New York: ReganBooks, 1998. Dominick struggles to understand who he is in the midst of his relationships, especially his relationship with his brother Thomas, a man suffering from schizophrenia.

Lionni, Leo. *Frederick*. New York: Pantheon, 1967. In this children's picture book, Frederick the mouse learns that the gift he offers is valuable to the community.

Malone, Michael. *Handling Sin*. New York: Pocket Books, 1986. In this novel, Raleigh Whittier Hayes embarks on a journey to rescue his father and ultimately reconnects with both God and himself.

Morrison, Toni. *The Bluest Eye*. New York: A Plume Book, 1970. Pecola prays for her eyes to become blue, so that she might be accepted and loved, just like the popular blue-eyed blond-haired children.

Sarton, May. *The Education of Harriet Hatfield*. New York: W. W. Norton & Company, 1989. After the death of her long-time partner, Harriet opens a feminist bookstore. In the process she comes to terms with who she is.

Winterson, Jeanette. *Oranges Are Not the Only Fruit*. New York: Grove Press, 1985. Winterson's autobiographical novel tells the tale of an orphan adopted into an evangelical household in northern England who must come to terms with her unorthodox sexuality.

Joy

Ackerman, Diane. *Cultivating Delight: A Natural History of My Garden*. New York: HarperCollins, 2001. Ackerman writes about how she nourishes her soul and cultivates delight by managing and nurturing her garden.

Kasl, Charlotte Davis. *Finding Joy: 101 Ways to Free Your Spirit and Dance with Life*. New York: HarperCollins, 1994. Kasl, a psychologist, offers concrete exercises and activities for cultivating joy.

Lewis, Sara. *The Answer Is Yes*. New York: Harcourt, 1998. Jenny feels lost after a move to San Diego for her husband Todd's career as a scientist. She begins to find the answers she needs when she happens upon a community learning center with the motto, "the answer is yes."

Leadership

Covey, Stephen. *The Seven Habits of Highly Effective People*. New York: A Fireside Book from Simon and Schuster, 1989. This book provides practical help for leaders who want to set priorities and make the best use of their time and resources.

Elliott, William. *Tying Rocks to Clouds: Meetings and Conversations with Wise and Spiritual People*. Wheaton, Ill.: Quest Books, 1995. This is a book of interviews with famous spiritual leaders from several faith traditions.

Farber-Robertson, Anita, Meredith Brook Handspicker, and David Whiman. *Learning While Leading: Increasing Your Effectiveness in Ministry*. Bethesda, Md.: The Alban Institute, 2000. This book uses case studies to present techniques to help religious professionals lead more effectively.

Heifetz, Ronald A. *Leadership without Easy Answers*. Cambridge, Mass.: Belknap Press, 1994. Heifetz, a professor at the John F. Kennedy School of Government, draws on dozens of years of research among leaders of business and politics to present strategies for leading.

Stevens, R. Paul, and Phil Collins. *The Equipping Pastor: A Systems Approach to Congregational Leadership*. Bethesda, Md.: The Alban Institute, 1993. The authors explain how understanding congregations as relational systems can aid the religious professional in leading.

Learning

www.faithandwisdom.org. Lifelong Learning Opportunities is a ministry of the Episcopal Church USA, the Evangelical Lutheran Church in America, and the United Methodist Church. Their Web site offers a list of theological and spiritual learning opportunities.

www.fishersnet.net. This online resource is sponsored by organizations connected to the Evangelical Lutheran Church in America and offers online theological education opportunities.

www.mindedge.com. This resource provides a database of information from a large number of learning centers for individuals interested in distance learning, continuing education, and training courses.

www.ncsu.edu. Richard M. Felder and Linda K. Silverman developed this instrument to test learning styles. The user can take the test and receive a score that summarizes one's individual learning styles. When you get to the NCSU home page, click on "Search" and enter the words, "Index of Learning Styles." Click on "Index of Learning Styles Questionnaire" and then follow the prompts to take the test.

www.osiem.org. This Web site provides spiritual resources for individuals and communities. It offers book reviews, discussion boards, and a calendar for learning opportunities.

DePorter, Bobbi, and Mike Hernacki. *Quantum Pathways: Discovering Your Personal Learning Style*. Oceanside, Calif.: Learning Forum, 2000. The authors provide information and tests to help readers discover their own style of learning.

Gardner, Howard. *Frames of Mind: The Theory of Multiple Intelligences*. New York: Basic Books, 1993. This is Gardner's ground-breaking work on his theory of multiple intelligences, which poses the existence of a number of ways of being intelligent.

Legacy

www.volunteermatch.org. This organization matches volunteers with opportunities for service.

Editors of Conari Press. *More Random Acts of Kindness*. Berkeley, Calif.: Conari Press, 1994.

———. *Random Acts of Kindness*. Berkeley, Calif.: Conari Press, 1993. Stories from people all over the world reflect the legacy we leave behind each day when we perform small and large acts of kindness towards strangers and friends.

Graham, Katharine. *Personal History*. New York: Vintage Books, 1998. Graham overcame many obstacles, including her husband's suicide, to succeed in life. After her husband's death, Graham went on to become the publisher of the *Washington Post*.

Harris, Jill Werman. *Remembrances and Celebrations: A Book of Eulogies, Elegies, Letters, and Epitaphs*. New York: Pantheon Books,

1999. This collection of remembrances provides touching examples of this genre from the pens of many famous persons.

Karon, Jan. *Miss Fannie's Hat*. Minneapolis: Augsburg Books, 1998. In this children's picture book, Miss Fannie donates her favorite hat to the church and receives a flower garden in return.

Kita, Joe. *Another Shot: How I Relived My Life in Less Than a Year*. Emmaus, Pa.: Rodale Press, 2001. Kita chose 25 regrets and attempted to reverse them in a course of a year.

L'Engle, Madeleine. *A Ring of Endless Light*. New York: Dell Publishing, 1980. In this young adult novel, Vicky Austin must come to terms with the dying of her beloved grandfather, a new relationship, and a spiritual encounter with the dolphins.

Polacco, Patricia. *Pink and Say*. New York: Philomel Books, 1994. This children's picture book is based on a true incident in the author's family history involving the friendship between a young white boy and a young black boy during the Civil War. Say survives to tell the story of their amazing friendship.

Ryan, M. J. *The Giving Heart: Unlocking the Transformative Power of Generosity in Your Life*. Berkeley, Calif.: Conari Press, 2000. These essays explain how giving time, energy, forgiveness, kindness, and helpful words can matter more than money.

Sachar, Louis. *Holes*. New York: Farrar, Straus, and Giroux, 1998. Stanley Yelnats ends up at a juvenile detention center as a result of a miscarriage of justice and while there discovers his destiny.

Sarton, May. *A Reckoning*. New York: W. W. Norton & Company, Inc., 1978. Laura Spelmen receives a terminal cancer diagnosis and uses her remaining time to let go of unessential matters and focus on the important connections in her life.

Seuss, Dr. *Oh, The Places You'll Go!* New York: Random House, 1990. This is a whimsical picture book about life's many possibilities.

Shulevitz, Uri. *The Treasure*. New York: Farrar, Straus, and Giroux, 1978. This picture book illustrates how sometimes one must travel far to find the treasure that is near.

Yancey, Philip. *Soul Survivor: How My Faith Survived the Church*. New York: Doubleday, 2001. Yancey profiles 13 individuals who have helped him to maintain his faith in God even when the church has abused and disappointed him.

Life Planning

Beck, Martha. *Finding Your Own North Star: Claiming the Life You Were Meant to Live*. New York: Crown Publishers, 2001. Beck offers helpful exercises for individuals who want to live more authentically.

Bolles, Richard N. *The Three Boxes of Life: An Introduction to Life/ Work Planning*. Berkeley, Calif.: The Ten Speed Press, 1981. Bolles takes the three boxes of education, work, and recreation and encourages readers to plan a life that includes all three all of the time.

Cooney, Barbara. *Miss Rumphius*. New York: Puffin Books, 1982. In this children's picture book, Miss Rumphius meets her father's challenge: to make the world a more beautiful place.

Fortgang, Laura Berman. *Living Your Best Life*. New York: Jeremy P. Tarcher/Putnam, 2001. Fortgang (www.laurabermanfortgang.com), a life and career coach, presents a 10-step system for excavating one's life blueprint.

Lloyd, Carol. *Creating a Life Worth Living*. New York: HarperPerennial, 1997. Lloyd's book, written for artists and innovators, offers tools for those who would like to create a unique career path.

Melander, Rochelle, and Harold Eppley. *Smart Choices: Making Your Way through Life*. Minneapolis: Augsburg Fortress, 1998. This small-group guide directs a group through the process of writing a personal mission statement.

Richardson, Cheryl. *Life Makeovers*. New York: Broadway Books, 2000. Coach Cheryl Richardson (www.cherylrichardson.com) provides 52 weeks of exercises geared at helping the reader improve his or her life.

———. *Take Time for Your Life*. New York: Broadway Books, 1998. Coach Cheryl Richardson presents a process to help the reader set priorities and make better life choices.

Meditation and Visualization

www.umass.edu/cfm/mbsr. This is the site for the Center for Mindfulness in Medicine, Healthcare, and Society. It is an outgrowth of Jon Kabat-Zinn's Stress Reduction Clinic and teaches Mindfulness Based Stress Reduction (MBSR). This site offers a helpful guide to locations that teach MBSR.

Gawain, Shakti. *Creative Visualization*. Toronto: Bantam Books, 1978. This is a classic introduction and workbook for the art of visualization.

Kabat-Zinn, Jon. *Wherever You Go There You Are: Mindfulness Meditation in Daily Life*. New York: Hyperion, 1994. Kabat-Zinn, the founder of the Stress Reduction Clinic at the University of Massachusetts Medical Center, presents a guide to use mindfulness meditation in daily life.

Monaghan, Patricia, and Eleanor G. Viereck. *Meditation: The Complete Guide*. Novato, Calif.: New World Library, 1999. This book provides more than 50 meditation styles and a self-test for determining which style is right for you.

Shafer, Kathryn, and Fran Greenfield. *Asthma Free in 21 Days: The Breakthrough Mindbody Healing Program*. San Francisco: HarperSanFrancisco, 2000. The authors provide a helpful program of journaling and creative visualization to aid asthma sufferers in improving their health. The book offers a special section for children. The exercises in this book, with some modification, could be helpful to people suffering from other chronic illnesses.

Wuellner, Flora Slosson. *Prayer and Our Bodies*. Nashville: The Upper Room, 1987. Wuellner uses prayer and guided meditation to teach readers how to listen to their bodies.

Midlife Transitions

Hardin, Paula Payne. *What Are You Doing with the Rest of Your Life: Choices in Midlife*. Novato, Calif.: New World Library, 1992. This book considers midlife changes and provides keys for living a generative life at any age.

Kidd, Sue Monk. *When the Heart Waits: Spiritual Direction for Life's Sacred Questions*. San Francisco: HarperSanFrancisco, 1990. In this memoir, Kidd tells the story of how God was present to her during transition in midlife.

Ministry

www.barna.org. This site offers current statistics on ministry, clergy, and congregations.

Antal, James M. *Considering a New Call: Ethical and Spiritual Challenges for Clergy*. Bethesda, Md.: The Alban Institute, 2000. Antal presents a helpful guide for clergy seeking a new call and desiring to maintain a healthy ministry throughout the process.

Cather, Willa. *Death Comes for the Archbishop*. New York: Vintage Books, 1990. In this novel, set in nineteenth-century New Mexico, Father Jean Marie Latour confronts loneliness as he ministers to the native population.

Clayton, Paul C. *Letters to Lee: Mentoring the New Minister*. Bethesda, Md.: The Alban Institute, 1999. This book, written as letters from a seasoned minister to a new clergy person, covers many of the new tasks that ministers face in their first call.

Crafton, Rev. Barbara Cawthorne. *The Sewing Room: Uncommon Reflection on Life, Love, and Work*. Harrisburg, Pa.: Morehouse Publishing, 1997. These essays by an Episcopal priest reflect on God's presence in her ministry and ordinary life.

Erdrich, Louise. *The Last Report on the Miracles at Little No Horse*. New York: HarperCollins, 2001. Father Damien Modeste has long served his people, the Ojibwe, on the distant reservation of Little No Horse. Nearing the end of his career, he dreads the discovery of his true identity—for he is a woman who has lived as a man.

Godwin, Gail. *Evensong*. New York: Ballantine Books, 1999.

———. *Father Melancholy's Daughter*. New York: William Morrow and Company, Inc., 1991. These two novels follow Margaret Gower. In the first, she and her father, an Episcopal priest, struggle with Margaret's mother's desertion. In the second, Pastor Margaret Gower ministers in her own small congregation.

Graham, Rev. Billy. *Just As I Am*. New York: HaperCollins, 1999. In this moving autobiography, Graham tells the story of his journey from his youth as a farm boy to his days as one of the world's best known preachers.

Hightower, James E. Jr., and W. Craig Gilliam. *A Time for Change: Re-Visioning Your Call*. Bethesda, Md.: The Alban Institute, 2000. This book offers suggestions and questions for clergy considering a career change.

Lawson, Kevin E. *How to Thrive in Associate Staff Ministry*. Bethesda, Md.: The Alban Institute, 2000. Lawson presents evidence that associate staff ministry is a calling with its own identity, integrity, and exciting possibilities.

Lindvall, Michael. *The Good News from North Haven*. New York: Doubleday and Company, Inc., 1991. This series of stories features a small-town Minnesota pastor as he confronts the challenges of parish ministry and life in a small community.

Nouwen, Henri M. *The Living Reminder: Service and Prayer in Memory of Jesus Christ*. San Francisco: HarperSanFrancisco, 1984. Nouwen writes about how Jesus' life and ministry can form the framework for our own ministry.

Peterson, Eugene H. *Working the Angles: The Shape of Pastoral Integrity*. Grand Rapids: William B. Eerdmans Publishing Company, 1987. Peterson encourages spiritual leaders to make prayer, scripture, and spiritual direction priorities in their ministry.

Phillips, Roy D. *Letting Go: Transforming Congregations for Ministry*. Bethesda, Md.: The Alban Institute, 1999. This book explains what it means for pastors to do less so that their members have the opportunity to grow their own abilities to serve.

Pym, Barbara. *Crampton Hodnet*. New York: A Plume Book, 1986. A gem from an author known for her dry wit as she characterizes British village life. In this novel, a priest in a small British village learns that his private life is not so private.

Secombe, Fred. *Chronicles of a Curate: How Green Was My Curate, A Curate for All Seasons, Goodbye Curate*. London: Fount Paperbacks, 1997.

————. *Chronicles of a Vicar: Hello Vicar!, A Comedy of Clerical Errors, The Crowning Glory*. London: Fount Paperbacks, 1999. Secombe's six-volume memoir of his days in the ministry begins in the Welsh valley at the close of the Second World War. The books read like fiction and contain situations familiar to most spiritual leaders.

Sittler, Joseph. *Gravity and Grace: Reflections and Provocations*. Minneapolis: Augsburg Publishing House, 1986. Linda-Marie Delloff, columnist for *The Lutheran*, edited this collection of Sittler's writings. The work covers his ideas on a broad range of topics, including ministry.

Sitze, Bob. *Not Trying Too Hard: New Basics for Sustainable Congregations*. Bethesda, Md.: The Alban Institute, 2001. Sitze advocates a "small-step approach" to congregational change and provides readers with the tools to take these steps.

Organizing

www.organizedhome.com. A Web site with organizing tips for each room.

Morgenstern, Julia. *Organizing from the Inside Out*. New York: Henry Holt and Company, 1998. The author provides an easy-to-follow process for clearing out extra stuff and organizing your space. Visit her Web site, www.juliemorgenstern.com, for more information.

Stewart, Martha. *Good Things for Organizing*. New York: Clarkson Potter/ Publishers, 2001. This book contains photos showing how to organize various rooms in the house, hints for creating organized spaces, and shopping information for the items demonstrated in the photos.

Retreats

www.recreation.gov. Search for a recreation site by activity, agency, or location.

Jones, Timothy K. *A Place for God: A Guide to Spiritual Retreats and Retreat Centers*. New York: Doubleday and Company, 2000. Jones describes a variety of retreat centers and includes helpful information on topics as varied as one's packing list and why one might choose to go on retreat.

Kelly, Jack, and Marcia Kelly. *Sanctuaries: The Complete United States*. New York: Crown Publishing Group, 1996. This guide lists many of the places available for retreats in the United States.

Louden, Jennifer. *The Woman's Retreat Book*. San Francisco: HarperSanFrancisco, 1997. Louden presents ideas for retreats in a variety of lengths and settings for women seeking to live more authentically. She includes helpful lists of books and films.

Miller, Jenifer. *Healing Centers and Retreats: Healthy Getaways for Every Body and Budget*. Emeryville, Calif.: Avalon Travel Publishing, 1998. This book provides information on spas and other health centers across the United States and Canada. The book includes a list that matches ailments to centers (for example, migraines).

Smith, Carol Ann, Eugene F. Merz, and Donald Doll. *Moment by Moment: A Retreat in Everyday Life*. Notre Dame, Ind.: Ave Maria Press, 2000. A collection of prayer exercises inspired by St. Ignatius of Loyola and designed to provide the reader with moments of retreat in a normal day.

Tidbury, Jane, and Peter Aprahamian. *Little Retreats*. New York: Crown Publishing Group, 2001. A coffee table book of personal retreat settings.

Sabbath

Bass, Dorothy. *Receiving the Day: Christian Practices for Opening the Gift of Time*. San Francisco: Jossey-Bass, 1999. Bass invites readers to understand time as God's blessing instead of a curse.

Bullock, A. Richard, and Richard J. Bruesehoff. *Clergy Renewal: The Alban Guide to Sabbatical Planning*. Bethesda, Md.: The Alban

Institute, 2000. The authors provide the definitive guide to putting together refreshing pastoral sabbaticals.

Edwards, Tilden. *Sabbath Time: Understanding and Practice for Contemporary Christians.* Nashville: Upper Room, 1992. Edwards writes about balancing the various parts of life: worship, play, rest, work, community, and ministry.

Heschel, Abraham Joshua. *The Sabbath.* New York: The Noonday Press, 1979. Heschel's classic work provides a helpful meditation on the Jewish understanding of Sabbath.

Muller, Wayne. *Sabbath: Finding Rest, Renewal, and Delight in Our Busy Lives.* New York: Bantam Doubleday Dell, 2000. Muller offers stories, poems, and suggestions for practicing the ancient tradition of Sabbath in our modern, busy lives.

Oswald, Roy. *Why You Should Give Your Pastor a Sabbatical.* Bethesda, Md.: The Alban Institute, 2001. Videocassette. Roy Oswald, author of *Clergy Self-Care: Finding a Balance for Effective Ministry*, presents a compelling argument that a sabbatical is an excellent strategy to help pastors maintain vitality in their work. The video is directed toward lay leaders.

Thurston, Bonnie. *To Everything a Season: The Spirituality of Time.* New York: Crossroad/Herder & Herder, 1999. A collection of essays that reflects on the mystery of time: its history, language, theology, seasons, and its place in our lives. It includes exercises to help readers understand their use of time.

Safety

www.cpsc.gov. This Web site belongs to the Consumer Product Safety Commission and provides helpful steps for improving the safety of one's home.

www.nsc.org. This is the home of the National Safety Council. It offers resources on safety, health, and environmental issues and provides an online library for consumers.

www.poison.org. This National Poison Control center offers poison prevention and first aid information.

www.safekids.org. The National Safe Kids Campaign provides safety tips for parents on a variety of issues from car seats to home hazards.

Self-Care

Domar, Alice D. *Self Nurture: Learning to Care for Yourself as Effectively as You Care for Everyone Else*. New York: Penguin USA, 2001. The director of the Mind/Body Center for Women's Health at Harvard Medical School presents a comprehensive year-long program to help women care for themselves.

Hands, Donald R., and Wayne L. Fehr. *Spiritual Wholeness for Clergy: A New Psychology of Intimacy with God, Self, and Others*. Bethesda, Md.: The Alban Institute, 1994. The authors combine clinical psychology and spiritual direction to create a practical model for spiritual wholeness.

Oswald, Roy M. *Clergy Self-Care: Finding a Balance for Effective Ministry*. Bethesda, Md.: The Alban Institute, 1991. This book uses self-assessment tools and examples from ministry to encourage clergy to balance self-care with ministry.

Self-Esteem

Cushman, Karen. *Catherine, Called Birdy*. New York: Harper Trophy, 1994. In this comical young adult novel set in the Middle Ages, Catherine learns to appreciate being herself.

Huber, Cheri. *There Is Nothing Wrong with You: Going Beyond Self-Hate*. Murphys, Calif.: Keep It Simple Books, 1993. Cheri Huber, a teacher of Zen, writes passionately about why we hate ourselves and how we can begin to love ourselves.

Reilly, Patricia Lynn. *Be Full of Yourself! The Journey from Self-Criticism to Self-Celebration*. Gualala, Calif.: Open Window Creations, 1997. Reilly, who earned her master of divinity degree from Princeton, approaches this topic from a theological perspective. Reilly includes helpful rituals, exercises, and instructions for group use.

————. *Imagine a Woman in Love with Herself: Embracing Your Wisdom and Wholeness*. Berkeley, Calif.: Conari Press, 1999. Through poetry, prayers, essays, and rituals, Reilly encourages women to love themselves.

Sexuality

www.religiousinstitute.org. This is the Web site of the Religious Institute on Sexuality, Morality, Justice, and Healing. It was founded in 2001 to promote their declaration on Sexual Morality, Justice and Healing, which has been signed by over 2,000 religious leaders. The site's best feature is its links to other organizations with projects on sexuality and religion.

Lodge, David. *Souls and Bodies*. New York: Penguin Books, 1980. Lodge follows a group of friends from their college days until middle adulthood, marking their struggle to discover how to weave together their Catholic faith, their sexuality, and their daily lives.

Weber, Christin Lore. *Altar Music*. New York: Scribner, 2000. Explore with three generations of Minnesota women the connections between faith, artistic passion, and sexuality.

Simple Living

DeGrote-Sorenson, Barbara, and David Allen Sorenson. *Six Weeks to a Simpler Lifestyle*. Minneapolis: Augsburg Fortress, 1994. In this follow-up to their first book, the authors provide practical suggestions for living more simply in just six weeks.

————. *Tis a Gift to Be Simple: Embracing the Freedom of Living with Less*. Minneapolis: Augsburg Fortress, 1992. The authors share practical advice from their own experiences with living simply.

Luhrs, Janet. *The Simple Living Guide: A Sourcebook for Less Stressful, More Joyful Living*. New York: Broadway Books, 1997. This book offers tips for living simply in every area of one's life including money, food, and travel. Each chapter contains a helpful resource list.

St. James, Elaine. *Living the Simple Life: A Guide to Scaling Down and Enjoying More*. New York: Hyperion, 1996. This book is St. James's follow-up to her 1994 book, providing further reflection on how to simplify daily life.

————. *Simplify Your Life: 100 Ways to Slow Down and Enjoy the Things That Really Matter*. New York: Hyperion, 1994. St. James provides concrete ideas for those who want to live a simpler life.

Sleep

www.aasmnet.org. This is the home of the American Academy of Sleep Medicine in Rochester, Minnesota. The site provides information on sleep hygiene and sleep disorders.

www.sleepfoundation.org. The National Sleep Foundation, an independent nonprofit organization, was established in 1990 in order to improve public awareness of sleep and its necessity for health. They have three aims: education, research, and advocacy.

www.sleephomepages.org. This Web site provides publication information, a list of resources, discussion boards, and a link to organizations dedicated to sleep health. Lynne Lamberg has also put together an extensive bibliography about sleep with detailed reviews of each book (www.sleephomepages.org/books/authorlist.html).

DeVries, Linda. *Spiritual Nightlights: Meditations for the Middle of the Night*. Wheaton, Ill.: Harold Shaw Publishers, 1997. DeVries, a recovering insomniac, offers meditations, prayers, and suggestions for those who suffer from sleep disorders.

Wood, Audrey, and Don Wood. *The Napping House*. San Diego: Harcourt, 2000. The gentle rhythm of this playful children's picture book might lull you to sleep.

Solitude

Koller, Alice. *An Unknown Woman*. New York: Bantam Books, 1981. Thirty-seven year old writer and doctoral student Alice Koller travels to Nantucket in winter to discover herself. In this space, she is freed to find a vision for her life.

Salwak, Dale, ed. *The Wonders of Solitude*. Novato: New World Library, 1998. This collection of quotes introduces the reader to the many facets of solitude.

Shulman, Alix Kates. *Drinking the Rain*. New York, Penguin Books, 1995. In this engaging memoir, 50-year-old Shulman leaves her New York City writer's life to live alone on an island off the coast of Maine. In a cabin devoid of modern conveniences, Shulman discovers courage and independence within herself.

Spiritual Directors

www.findthedivine.com. This Web site offers links and information about retreat centers and spiritual directors.

www.sdiworld.org. The Web site for Spiritual Directors International, an organization for supporting and networking spiritual directors around the world. It is the home of Presence: The Journal of Spiritual Directors International. The Web site offers a helpful list of organizations that train spiritual directors.

www.shalem.org. The Web site for the Shalem Institute for Spiritual Formation, an ecumenical organization devoted to the teaching and support of contemplative spirituality. The institute provides an extensive study program for spiritual directors. The Web site contains Shalem News, filled with helpful articles about spirituality and spiritual direction.

Addison, Howard A. *Show Me Your Way: The Complete Guide to Exploring Interfaith Spiritual Direction.* Woodstock, Vt.: Skylight Paths Publishing, 2000. Rabbi Addison, a former student of Abraham Joshua Heschel, describes his experiences taking spiritual direction from directors of other faith traditions. The book includes a helpful resource list.

Dubay, Thomas. *Seeking Spiritual Direction: How to Grow the Divine Life Within.* Ann Arbor, Mich.: Servant Publications, 1994. This is a practical guide for Christians seeking a spiritual director. It explains spiritual direction, how to evaluate a potential director, how to find a director, and provides ideas for deepening one's prayer life.

Gratton, Carolyn. *The Art of Spiritual Guidance: A Contemporary Approach to Growing in the Spirit.* New York: Crossroad/Herder & Herder, 1993. This classic overview, written by a psychologist and professor of spirituality, provides helpful psychological insights about spiritual formation.

Jones, Alan W. *Exploring Spiritual Direction.* Cambridge, Mass.: Cowley Publications, 1999. Jones, the dean of Grace Cathedral in San Francisco, explores spiritual direction and spiritual friendship.

Leech, Kenneth. *Soul Friend.* Harrisburg, Pa.: Morehouse Publishing, 2001. Originally Published in 1977, this book is a classic exploration of the Christian practice of spiritual direction.

Spiritual Exercises and Tools

www.jesuit.ie/prayer. This is the home of Sacred Space, a daily prayer site run by the Irish Jesuits. It offers a daily prayer to be done at one's computer.

www.methodx.net. This Web site was created by Upper Room Ministries and offers an introduction to many of the tools of contemplative spirituality, as well as an opportunity to connect with other believers.

www.spiritualityhealth.com. This Web site, related to the magazine *Spirituality and Health*, features book reviews, movie reviews, e-courses, a listing of spirituality retreats, and a very helpful collection of links to religious sites.

Artress, Lauren. *Walking a Sacred Path: Rediscovering the Labyrinth as a Spiritual Tool.* New York: Berkley Publishing Group, 1990. The author, a psychotherapist and priest, explores the use of the labyrinth as a spiritual tool.

Barry, William A. *Finding God in All Things: A Companion to the Spiritual Exercises of St. Ignatius*. Notre Dame, Ind.: Ave Maria Press, 1991. Barry's book is a companion to St. Ignatius's spiritual exercises, which seeks to help the reader grow in relationship to God.

Brussat, Frederic, and Mary Ann Brussat. *Spiritual RX: Prescriptions for Living a Meaningful Life*. New York: Hyperion, 2000. This book offers spiritual exercises, reading lists, movie reviews, and recommendations for developing a personal spiritual practice.

Camp, Carole Ann, and Donna E. Schaper. *Labyrinths from the Outside In: Walking to Spiritual Insight, A Beginner's Guide*. Woodstock, Vt.: Skylight Paths Publications, 2000. This book is a user-friendly guide to making and walking the labyrinths. The book includes the history and philosophy of labyrinths as well as guides for use.

Melander, Rochelle, and Harold Eppley. *Dancing in the Aisle: Spiritual Lessons We've Learned from Children*. Cleveland: United Church Press, 1999. The authors reflect on how their encounters with children have taught them about spirituality. Each essay is accompanied by a Bible reading, questions for reflection, and a spiritual challenge.

Mundy, Linus. *The Complete Guide to Prayer-Walking: A Simple Path to Body-and-Soul Fitness*. New York: Crossroad Publishing Company, 1996. Mundy's book offers suggestions for meditations, prayers, and prayer-starters for the beginning prayer-walker.

Nelson, Gertrude Mueller. *To Dance with God: Family Ritual and Community Celebration*. New York: Paulist Press, 1986. Nelson's book follows the liturgical calendar and suggests meaningful ways for families and congregations to celebrate each season.

Reilly, Patricia Lynn. *A God Who Looks Like Me: Discovering a Woman-Affirming Spirituality*. New York: Ballantine Books, 1995. Reilly offers meditations and exercises centered around biblical women and religious stories as a way of helping modern women connect to God.

Rupp, Joyce. *The Star in My Heart: Experiencing Sophia, Inner Wisdom*. Philadelphia: Innisfree Press, 1990. Rupp, a member of the Servants of Mary community, presents essays, poems, and exercises designed to help the reader connect both to God and their own wisdom.

St. James, Elaine. *Inner Simplicity: 100 Ways to Regain Peace and Nourish Your Soul*. New York: Hyperion, 1995. St. James presents simple ideas for creating inner peace, such as smile a lot and find a teacher.

Wiederkehr, Macrina. *The Song of the Seed: A Monastic Way of Tending the Soil.* San Francisco: HarperSanFrancisco, 1995. A study centered around the parable of the sower that includes readings, prayers, and exercises.

Spiritual Life

Bradley, Marion Zimmer. *The Mists of Avalon.* New York: Ballantine Books, 1982. This is the tale of Sir Arthur and the knights of the round table, told from the women's point of view, and centered around the battle between the old spirituality and the rise of Christianity.

Diamant, Anita. *The Red Tent.* New York: Picador USA, 1997. The life of the biblical character Dinah is given form and substance in this historical novel. Diamant, who frequently writes about modern Jewish life, provides a keen vision of how the women of Dinah's day lived.

Fynn. *Mister God, This Is Anna.* New York: Ballantine, 1974. A little girl, Anna, teaches Fynn about God.

Goldberg, Myla. *Bee Season.* New York: Doubleday, 2000. When Ellie wins a spelling bee, it leads to an adventure in which all of the members of her Jewish family explore their spirituality.

Hansen, Ron. *Mariette in Ecstasy.* New York: HarperCollins, 1991. A passionately devout young woman, a postulant in a New York convent in 1906, appears to experience ecstatic encounters with the divine.

Potok, Chaim. *Davita's Harp.* New York: Fawcett Crest, 1985. Davita, raised by political activists who have abandoned the faiths of their childhood, must find her own spiritual path—even in the midst of tragedy.

Sweet, Leonard. *Learn to Dance the Soul Salsa: 17 Surprising Steps for Godly Living in the Twenty-first Century.* Grand Rapids: Zondervan Publishing House, 2000. Sweet presents practical lifestyle changes for Christians who want to live a spiritual life. Each chapter is packed with helpful quotes and ends with resources, questions, and exercises.

Spiritual Memoir and Essays

Album, Mitch. *Tuesdays with Morrie.* New York: Bantam Doubleday Dell, 1997. Album's account of his professor's last months reveals Morrie's wisdom about life.

Allende, Isabel. *Paula*. New York: HarperCollins, 1996. Allende's daughter became sick from a rare blood disease on her honeymoon and fell into a coma. Allende, writing at her daughter's bedside, tells the story of her life.

Angelou, Maya. *All God's Children Need Traveling Shoes*. New York: Vintage Books, 1986.

————. *Gather Together in My Name*. New York: Bantam Books, 1974.

————. *The Heart of a Woman*. New York: Bantam Books, 1981.

————. *I Know Why the Caged Bird Sings*. New York: Bantam Books, 1969.

————. *Singin' and Swingin' and Gettin' Merry Like Christmas*. New York: Bantam Books, 1976.

————. *Wouldn't Take Nothing for My Journey Now*. New York: Bantam Books, 1993. Angelou's series of memoirs is a moving testimony to the human ability to overcome obstacles and thrive.

Bender, Sue. *Plain and Simple: A Woman's Journey to the Amish*. San Francisco: HarperSanFrancisco, 1989. Bender lives with an Amish family, engaging in many aspects of Amish life. In the process, Bender learns about her own spiritual journey.

Benson, Robert. *Living Prayer*. New York: Putnam, 1999. Benson writes about his attempts to weave prayer into his daily schedule.

Bondi, Roberta. *Memories of God: Theological Reflections on a Life*. Nashville: Abingdon Press, 1995. Bondi reflects on how her own life's journey has led her to discover theological truths, such as the meaning of the incarnation.

Buechner, Frederick. *The Alphabet of Grace*. New York: Harper & Row Publishers, 1970. Buechner uses the alphabet as a metaphor as he seeks to understand the mysteries of God and God's ways.

DePree, Max. *Dear Zoe: Letters to My Grandchild on the Wonder of Life*. Grand Rapids: William B. Eerdmans, 1998. This memoir collects the author's letters to his premature granddaughter explaining his faith and the meaning of life.

Gallagher, Joan. *Things Seen and Unseen: A Year Lived by Faith*. New York: Alfred A. Knopf, 1998. Gallagher, an Episcopal laywoman, tells the story of a year in the life of her California congregation.

Hampl, Patricia. *Virgin Time: In Search of the Contemplative Life*. New York: Ballantine Books, 1992. Hampl tells of a pilgrimage she took in order to immerse herself in contemplative prayer.

Hansen, Ron. *A Stay against Confusion: Essays on Fiction and Faith*. New York: HarperCollins, 2001. Novelist Ron Hansen explores a variety of spiritual topics including the stigmata, prayer, and the Eucharist.

Henry, Patrick. *The Ironic Christian's Companion*. New York: Riverhead Books, 1999. Henry draws on the work of a variety of popular thinkers to present an imaginative look at the Christian faith.

Lamott, Anne. *Traveling Mercies: Some Thoughts on Faith*. New York: Pantheon Books, 1999. Lamott's ruthlessly honest and often humorous essays reflect on her journey to and within Christianity.

L'Engle, Madeleine. *A Circle of Quiet*. New York: Farrar, Straus, and Giroux, 1972.

————. *The Irrational Season*. New York: The Seabury Press, 1977.

————. *The Summer of the Great Grandmother*. New York: Farrar, Straus, and Giroux, 1974.

————. *Two-Part Invention: The Story of a Marriage*. New York: Farrar, Straus, and Giroux, 1988. L'Engle, best known for her fiction for young readers, writes about her life as a wife and mother and her struggles to live a Christian life.

McCourt, Frank. *Angela's Ashes*. New York: Scribner 1996. McCourt's humorous and moving tale portrays his youth in Ireland.

Nesaule, Agate. *A Woman in Amber: Healing the Trauma of War and Exile*. New York: Penguin, 1995. This moving memoir reflects on Nesaule's childhood escape from Latvia during the Second World War and her subsequent emigration to America.

Peterson, Eugene. *The Wisdom of Each Other*. Grand Rapids: Zondervan Publishing House, 1998. Peterson illustrates the life-changing value of spiritual friendships in this collection of letters to a fictional friend.

Wiesel, Elie. *Night*. New York: Bantam Doubleday Dell, 1982. Wiesel recounts his experiences as a child in a Nazi death camp.

Wolf, Molly. *Hiding in Plain Sight: Sabbath Blessings*. Collegeville, Minn.: The Liturgical Press, 1998. These essays ponder God's presence in the work and objects of ordinary life.

Spirituality and Place
Gruchow, Paul. *The Necessity of Empty Places*. Minneapolis: Milkweed Editions, 1999. Gruchow's essays on nature reflect on his own wilderness experiences.

Norris, Kathleen. *Dakota*. New York: Ticnor & Fields, 1993. Norris, a
   poet, writes of returning to the house built by her grandparents in South
   Dakota and how both the land and the people have shaped her spirituality.
Sweetland, Nancy. *God's Quiet Things*. Grand Rapids: William B.
   Eerdmans, 1994. In this picture book, the reader is introduced to the
   quiet ways in which God is present to the world.

Spirituality and Writing
Klug, Ron. *How to Keep a Spiritual Journal: A Guide to Journal Keeping
   for Inner Growth and Personal Discovery*. Minneapolis: Augsburg
   Fortress, 2002. This guide provides several options for using journal
   writing as a tool for spiritual growth.
Lamott, Anne. *Bird by Bird: Reflections on Writing and Life*. New York:
   Pantheon Books, 1994. Lamott's often humorous reflections about the
   writing life apply well to the tasks inherent in both life and ministry.
L'Engle, Madeleine. *Walking on Water: Reflections on Faith and Art*.
   Wheaton, Ill.: Harold Shaw Publishers, 2000. L'Engle meditates on
   what it means to be both a Christian and an artist.
O'Connor, Flannery. *Mystery and Manners*. New York: Farrar, Straus,
   and Giroux, 1957. O'Connor, known for her short stories, writes essays
   about the connection between faith and fiction.

Staff Support
Oswald, Roy M. *Why You Should Develop a Pastor-Parish Relations
   Committee*. Bethesda, Md.: The Alban Institute, 2001. Videocassette.
   Roy Oswald explains that the sole task of this committee (sometimes
   called a staff support committee) should be to monitor the quality of
   the relationship between the pastor and the congregation.
Rubietta, Jane. *How to Keep the Pastor You Love*. Downer's Grove, Ill.:
   InterVarsity Press, 2002. This book is a proactive and encouraging
   tool that delves into the roles, responsibilities, and relationships of both
   congregation and clergy. Each chapter provides practical applications
   for both the congregation and the pastor.

Time Management
Morgenstern, Julie. *Time Management from the Inside Out*. New York:
   Henry Holt and Company, 2000. The organization guru takes on time
   management in this practical guide to ordering your days
   (www.juliemorgenstern.com).

Vision

Buechner, Frederick. *Godric*. San Francisco: Harper and Row Publishers, 1980. This is a fictional account of Godric of Finchale, a holy man from the twelfth century.

Follett, Ken. *The Pillars of the Earth*. New York: A Plume Book, 1989. This historical novel is the story of individuals with the vision of building a great cathedral.

Irving, John. *A Prayer for Owen Meany*. New York: William Morrow and Company, 1989. Owen Meany has an absolutely clear vision for his life. Johnny, the novel's narrator, tells the story of that vision and the events that unfold from it. He attributes his belief in Christ to Meany's presence in his life.

Williams, Niall, and Christine Breen. *O Come Ye Back to Ireland: Our First Year in County Clare*. New York: SoHo Press, 1987. A young American couple travels from New York to a farm in the west of Ireland to start a new life.

Vocation and Work

www.jobhuntersbible.com. This Web site is designed to be a supplement to Richard Bolles's book *What Color Is Your Parachute?* One of the site's best features is the links to other sites for job hunters.

Bolles, Richard Nelson. *What Color Is Your Parachute? 2001: A Practical Manual for Job-Hunters and Career-Changers*. Berkeley, Calif.: Ten Speed Press, 2000. Bolles, a spiritual leader himself, has created a self-help book packed with a variety of tools for those who want to change their jobs. He includes a list of counseling centers that work with clergy.

Galdone, Paul. *The Little Red Hen*. New York: Houghton Mifflin, 1984. Revisit this classic children's tale about not wanting to take responsibility for work.

―――. *The Three Little Pigs*. New York: Houghton Mifflin, 1991. A trio of swine learn about how the quality of one's work can affect one's life in this well-known story for children.

Palmer, Parker J. *The Active Life: A Spirituality of Work, Creativity, and Caring*. San Francisco: Jossey-Bass, 1999. Using stories from a variety of religious traditions, Palmer contemplates the spirituality of working.

————. *Let Your Life Speak: Listening for the Voice of Vocation*. San Francisco: Jossey-Bass, 1999. A Quaker and educator, Palmer's essays about his own attempt to hear the voice of vocation provide wisdom and inspiration.

Paterson, Katherine. *Lyddie*. New York: Penguin Putnam Books for Young Readers, 1994. In this novel for middle grade readers, Lyddie Warthen, a Vermont farm girl, works in a factory in Lowell, Massachusetts.

Salzman, Mark. *The Soloist*. New York: Vintage Books, 1995. A gifted musician's vocation is tested when he loses the ability to perform.

See, Carolyn. *The Handyman*. New York: Ballantine, 2000. A painter, before he becomes famous, takes on various "handyman" jobs to fund his painting and appears to have a vocation for caring for others.

Tyler, Anne. *A Patchwork Planet*. New York: Alfred A. Knopf, 1998. In this novel, Barnaby lives his discipleship as he cares for the elderly and infirm through his job at Rent-a-Back, Inc.

Whitney, Catherine A. *The Calling: A Year in the Life of an Order of Nuns*. New York: Crown Publishers, 1999. A memoir that reflects on Whitney's calling to the convent and her life inside its walls.

Wisdom

Carlstrom, Nancy White. *Does God Know How to Tie Shoes?* Grand Rapids: William B. Eerdmans Publishing Company, 1993. Words and messages about God come from wise parents in response to a child's questions in this picture book for young children.

Franklin, Kristine. *The Old, Old Man a nd the Very Little Boy*. New York: Atheneum, 1992. This picture book portrays an emotional relationship between a wise elder and a young boy in an African village.

Ruiz, Don Miguel. *The Four Agreements: A Toltec Wisdom Book*. San Rafael, Calif.: Amber-Allen Publishing, 1997. Ruiz's book centers around four agreements: be impeccable with your word, don't take anything personally, don't make assumptions, and always do your best.